EVENTS AND THE SOCIAL SCIENCES

As the events management field expands as an area of study, there is a need to move beyond the business- and marketing-driven approaches which dominate the literature towards a more advanced conceptual analysis and understanding of events from a socio-cultural context.

This book addresses this need by examining intersections between the social sciences and the emerging field of events management. It applies and specifically contextualises social science theories within the discourse of events to provide a greater understanding of the significance of events in contemporary society. It first outlines the value of approaching the study of events from a social science perspective, and then moves on to an in-depth exploration of relevant theories exploring topics such as identity, culture, consumerism, representation and place. It concludes with a summary of each chapter and a discussion of ways in which events can be further explored through the lens of the social sciences.

The book features international case studies based on a variety of event types ranging from sports events, religious and cultural events, and community events, which are used throughout to address contemporary issues and show theory in practice. 'Think Points' are integrated into each chapter to encourage the reader to reflect on theories, and each chapter concludes with summary points, further reading and links to useful websites to consolidate learning and further knowledge.

This book will provide upper-level students, academics and researchers interested in events, as well as those from related social science disciplines, with a robust socio-cultural conceptual analysis of the subject and a greater understanding of the significance of events in contemporary society.

Hazel Andrews is Senior Lecturer in Tourism, Culture and Society in the Centre for Tourism, Event and Food Studies at Liverpool John Moores University.

Teresa Leopold is Senior Lecturer in Tourism and Event Management Studies in the Business School at the University of Sunderland.

EVENTS AND THE SOCIAL SCIENCES

Hazel Andrews and Teresa Leopold

First published 2013
by Routledge
2 Park Square, Milton Park, Abingdon, Oxon OX14 4RN

Simultaneously published in the USA and Canada
by Routledge
711 Third Avenue, New York, NY 10017

Routledge is an imprint of the Taylor & Francis Group, an informa business

British Library Cataloguing in Publication Data
A catalogue record for this book is available from the British Library

Library of Congress Cataloging in Publication Data
Andrews, Hazel.
 Events and the social sciences / Hazel Andrews and Teresa Leopold.
 — 1st ed.
  p. cm.
 Includes bibliographical references and index.
 1. Special events—Management. 2. Social sciences. I. Leopold, Teresa.
 II. Title.
 GT3405.A64 2013
 394.2—dc23
                                2012029311

ISBN: 978-0-415-60560-1 (hbk)
ISBN: 978-0-415-60562-5 (pbk)
ISBN: 978-0-203-07074-1 (ebk)

Typeset in Bembo
by Keystroke, Station Road, Codsall, Wolverhampton

Printed and bound in Great Britain by the MPG Books Group

CONTENTS

FIGURES

TABLES

CASE STUDIES

ACKNOWLEDGEMENTS

We would like to express our thanks and gratitude to the following people for their help and support during the writing of this book:

Professor Jeremy Boissevain for his advice in the early stages of writing.

Dr Jan Mosedale and Dr Les Roberts for useful discussions, comments on drafts of the manuscript and help with photos.

Martha Noyes for her assistance with photographs.

1

INTRODUCTION

Events are based in society and involve people. They comprise interactions between people and places and they have costs and benefits. As such there is a need to understand the dynamics of the world in which events are situated and to which they contribute. We believe that this must go beyond the 'how to' tool-kit approach of a management degree, regardless of the importance of the practical skills such courses provide. The burgeoning of events management courses in the UK and the emerging profession of events management globally in recent years (Harris and Huyskens 2001) responds to the increasing number of 'events' in society at large (see for example Boissevain 1992, 2008; Guiu 2008; Kooistra 2011; Gibson and Connell 2011). However, the study of events is nothing new as many disciplines and other fields of studies have used event contexts to gain a deeper understanding of their own area. For example, the field of tourism has long focused on the role of events in attracting tourists by adding to the cultural offer of destinations. Indeed, the text by Greenwood (1989) is based around an examination of the Alarde festival in the Basque region of Spain. Although Greenwood's central discussion on the development of a local festival into a tourist attraction has been subject to much debate in the field of tourism studies, his work, which illuminates the intersection between people, place, politics and commercial interests, is based in the context of a public event. In addition there is much academic literature on the subject of events to be found in the tourism studies journals, among other areas of study – see for example Getz (2007, 2012), who acknowledges that events are linked to not only specific areas of study, for instance performance studies, but also embedded in major academic disciplines including, for example, social anthropology, sociology and cultural geography.

The inspiration for this book came from both of our interactions with events management programmes at universities based in the UK. We have observed that events management students struggle not only with drawing links between the events and tourism sectors (and other related sectors) but also with the socio-cultural context of events. We both come from a social science based tourism studies background and we understand that many of the issues that underpin the management of anything need to be informed by insights on the social and cultural world found in the social sciences. We want to enrich the study of events and provide students with the opportunities to explore these aspects of their chosen area of study, and develop their critical and creative skills, which should underpin all aspects of university study for the betterment of society.

Our concern is the non-business aspects because often business elements have become over-privileged in the studies of events to date. We believe that one danger of a sole focus on managerial and business aspects of the studies of events is that it masks other areas of study relating to events, and often disregards events that cannot be planned, managed and exploited for economic purposes. As Jackson notes (2005: 1) 'The course of history, like the course of any human life, comprises a succession of turbulent events interrupted by periods of comparative calm.' There are occurrences in life that are unpredictable and can be life-changing, for example a car accident or violent attack. Such events do not fall under the remit of commercial-based sensibilities and, as such, the business focus of events appears to be concerned only with that which can be staged. Underpinning these orchestrated events is an unspoken ideology that perpetuates the need to manage, categorise and bureaucratise social interaction and influence social order. It appears to us that the main concern is with the commodification of existing rites and rituals and the development of economic enterprises.

The study of events

An event is a mix of elements that all overlap to inform event practices. Events happen at a specified place, they involve people of different socio-cultural backgrounds and incorporate elements of business practices (whether this might be a large-scale fundraising event or the organisation of a child's birthday party). Figure 1.1 demonstrates the links between the practice of events management and the socio-cultural and place elements that this book seeks to illuminate. All these aspects play a role in events and therefore studies of events should consider each of them. We believe that a comprehensive understanding of the nature of events can only be achieved by acknowledging all three features, which contribute to the making of an event regardless of its purpose.

In these opening paragraphs we have been using the word 'events' but in thinking through our approach to the studies of events for this book the word has perplexed us more and more and we have found ourselves challenging the meanings of the term. It is to this thorny issue that we now turn. If we look at dictionary definitions we find the following:

> happen, occurrence, an incident, any one of the possible occurrences which happens under stated conditions, an item in a sports programme, that which

FIGURE 1.1 The main features of the studies of events

results from a course of proceedings, a consequence, what becomes of a person or thing (fate), to come to pass, to expose to the air. (*Shorter Oxford English Dictionary* [*SOED*])

From this we can gather that in fact *anything* can be understood to be an event, something that happens or occurs. Therefore it is no surprise that the word has been used within management culture to describe a disparate range of activities without any clear justification or real definition. Jago and Shaw (1998) draw attention to the confusion within the events literature around the segmentation of events. They list the transposability of synonyms connected to the terms 'major event', 'special event' and 'hallmark event', and highlight that 'there is no consensus in the literature about the relationships between the various categories of events' (Jago and Shaw 1998: 25). In our view, the attempts to put meaning in the categories through identification of attributes are by their very nature relative and based on prerequisites which are themselves open to interpretation. For example, McDonnell (2003) lists qualities, which make up a 'special event' (such as having a festive spirit, being unique, being authentic) but clearly states that a special event does not have to have all of these features to be considered a 'special event'.

After all, an event is any act in the conduct of life. However, in terms of the increasing management culture associated with the advancement of a neoliberal political economy, in which the quantification and management of nearly all areas of the social world is a central project, it appears that all facets of social interaction and practice require a bureaucratic response and structure (Handelman 1998). This may be particularly so in the public arena, where groups of people united in a common cause may come together. Taking the UK as an example we have seen curbs in collective representation in all sorts of ways – from the eroding of trade union power to the restrictions on organised demonstrations.

THINK POINT

In the summer of 2011 in the UK there were a number of demonstrations or riots, which resulted in acts of civil disobedience including looting, arson and street battles with the police. Are these happenings an event and if so should they be part of your study at university?

Commonly used terminology found in the events literature such as 'mega event' and 'hallmark event' have developed with links to the contexts of globalisation, marketing and economics, and reflect the centrality of managerial approaches in studies of events. Conversely, the terms 'spectacle', 'festivals', 'carnivals', 'ceremonies' and 'parades' are rather applied to socio-cultural contexts within other areas of study and major academic disciplines. Thus, we would like to foreground the existing theoretical insights of the social sciences (e.g. ritual, consumption, ideas of performance) and (re-)introduce them into events management courses, and, as a result, encourage discussions and thinking about social science discourses in the studies of events, recognising that some of these issues are already being addressed in existing events curricula.

In other words, 'events' encompass all the occasions listed in Table 1.1, the study of which is deeply rooted in the socio sciences and can therefore provide firmer theoretical underpinnings for the complex dynamics that make up these things labelled 'events'. We list these terms and their dictionary definitions (*OED*) as a starting point to broaden the research terminology in events management and not to rely on a single all-encompassing word. To be clear, we are using 'events' in this book as a term which covers spectacle, rituals, festivals, carnivals, ceremonies and parades but does not refer to the common categorisation found within the events management discourse.

In our experience, events management students often struggle to recognise the linkage between their chosen course and other areas of study and academic disciplines. Thus, having emphasised the complexities and difficulties of understanding what an event is, we further need to situate the study of events in the social sciences

TABLE 1.1 Broadening event terminology

Terminology	Explanation
Spectacle	a visually striking performance or display; an event or scene regarded in terms of its visual impact
Ritual	a religious or solemn ceremony consisting of a series of actions performed according to a prescribed order[1]
Festival	a day or period of celebration, typically for religious reasons; an organised series of concerts, plays or films, typically one held annually in the same place
Ceremony	a formal religious or public occasion, especially one celebrating a particular event, achievement or anniversary; the ritual observances and procedures required or performed at grand and formal occasions
Carnival	an annual festival, typically during the week before Lent in Roman Catholic countries, involving processions, music, dancing and the use of masquerade; inversion[2]
Parade	a public procession, especially one celebrating a special day or event
Procession	a number of people or vehicles moving forward in an orderly fashion, especially as part of a ceremony
Celebration	the action of celebrating an important day or event

Notes
1 A ritual does not need to be solemn; see our discussion in chapter 3.
2 A carnival can also encompass the suspension of social norms.

as this will help students to better appreciate and recognise how their programme of study is embedded in wider research programmes and agendas. In the preceding discussion we drew attention to some links between the study of tourism and the emergence of the study of events. In addition, we can note that these things we call events are related to other areas of study, themselves underpinned by social science approaches.

To bring the focus back to the purpose of this book, its key theme is that events take place within a socio-cultural context and events managers must be sensitive to social science theories and issues, which affect the industry. Further, those engaged on an academic route to the understanding of events also need to appreciate the theoretical lineage to which some discussions and critiques are indebted, to ensure the effectiveness of their own research and outputs. To this end we have identified areas that appear to us to be informative in terms of an introduction to a social science understanding of events. The rest of this chapter provides an outline of the structure of the book.

Chapter outlines

We start in chapter 2 by considering the social significance of events. To do this we first think about the term 'society' – what it means and the relationship of the individual to it. We introduce the terms 'structure' and 'agency' to illuminate the complex nature of the interplay between individuals (agents) and the whole, or structures that help to inform actions and dispositions. We then examine the evolutionary nature of society by looking at the different stages of societal development that have been identified. These stages are the pre-modern, modern and postmodern eras and connect their characteristics to the different forms that events take in each period. In particular we look at some of the key characteristics and processes associated with modernity that have influenced the development and practice of varying types of events. We note that the modern phase is characterised by an increasing number of events both in Europe (Boissevain 1992, 2008) and the United States. The chapter introduces the work of Durkheim (1933) and Tönnies (1957) to help us understand the changes in social conditions and practices as society moved from a pre-modern to a modern state.

In chapter 3 we focus on ritual and rites of passage, for example celebrations such as birthdays and religious ceremonies. Theories relating to the understanding of ritual are important areas of study in the social sciences, particularly in social anthropology. They help us to explore how individuals and/or social groups understand their identities. Many happenings that are incorporated under the terminology of events can be understood as rituals or rites of passage, so there is much to be learned about their practice by considering social science perspectives. The chapter introduces the work of Arnold van Gennep (1960) on rituals as rites of passage, discussing the role of rituals as markers of life stages. Many personal events fall into the category of a rite that signals change in, for example, status; a wedding for instance acknowledges the change from being single to being married. We go on to think about how Victor Turner (1969) developed van Gennep's ideas, identifying that all rites involve three distinct phases, which are the pre-liminal, liminal and post-liminal stages. We also examine the ritual narratives and objects linked to rites. Although the foundation for many of the theories is a concern with religious practices, the ideas are nonetheless still relevant for occasions not grounded in religion and we identify a number of secular rituals. The development of these secular rituals often relies on trying to ground the event in a sense of tradition which at times does not stand up to historical scrutiny. To understand this dynamic further we consider the idea of invented traditions.

In chapter 4 we move on to the importance of performance to understandings of event consumers, narratives and experiences. We explore the term 'performance' and demonstrate that events are composed of a number of different performances and actors, including the audience and the 'players'. We also consider the event as a performance highlighting a series of steps that all events have in common. We introduce the work of Richard Schechner, who has written extensively on performance studies and whose work can be used to analyse the different ways in which events (and the same event) can be practised. In this chapter we also wish to draw attention to the ways in which not all events are planned but are still embedded in the social and cultural practices of the quotidian world. In this respect we look at the importance of the context in which actions take place. In so doing we highlight the need to consider the on-going to-and-fro between context, performers and audiences which means that understandings and practices associated with events are contingent rather than inherent in the event itself. Thus any predetermined ideas of what an event is about or how it should be performed can be overturned. Deighton's (1992) work on the categories of performance is introduced to further explore the different types of performances at an event. By firmly linking events to society we can also see how material representations of societal norms and ideas are used as part of events practices.

Moving on to chapter 5, we examine consumer society and the experience economy with particular focus on consumption. The chapter starts with definitions of 'consumption' and the development of the term to include activities that are not necessarily based on economic concerns. In terms of events we can think of an event as an item for consumption in its own right, but at the same time an event will include many consumption practices – or opportunities for such practices. Consumer culture is closely linked to the issue of commodification, a process by which many forms of cultural products and experiences are given a monetary value so that they can be sold. For many scholars this raises concerns about the authenticity of some aspects of material and non-material culture – are they genuine if mass produced or made with the purpose of economic gain rather than symbolic of religious belief for example? The importance of the symbolic value of things is then explored with particular reference to how artefacts and performances can be read as representations of identity. In terms of the experience economy, we draw attention to a quest for sensations, which is also packaged as part of events' products for consumption purposes but does not rely on material goods but rather the experience of the event. Thus what does it feel like – emotionally and bodily – to be at an event? The last section in the chapter looks at those events in which practices of consumption could be argued to have less of a central role. We look at giving, in order to think about events based on charitable purposes, non-commercial fundraising and sponsorship.

Chapter 6 examines the importance of place and representation in the making of events. We may think we know what we mean when we use words such as space, place and landscape but they are in fact open to interpretation and have been the subject of debates within and across different disciplinary boundaries. We therefore explore some different theoretical perspectives brought to bear on these terms and their relevance to events. From here we discuss the importance of a sense of place to the shaping of relations with, and experiences of, the varying physical scenarios in which events can be practised. A sense of place links to feelings of belonging and identity associated with particular places. There is often a desire to demonstrate such feelings and identifications, which may lead into certain types of event activities to demonstrate, for example, how a village or street fits into a region or neighbourhood. As such we can again see how factors that appear to be external to an event actually influence the form, participation in and experiences of what has occurred or is happening. Ideas of place and the feelings associated with them can act to exclude people as well as include them. We introduce the writings of Henri

Lefebvre (1991) to explore the relationships between the different aspects that produce space. Lefebvre identifies spatial practices, representations of space and spaces of representation. This theory highlights the connection between how a space is represented through, for example, maps, diagrams and marketing material, and how people live the space. By this we mean: do people accept the ideas of the space as it is represented or does their behaviour challenge these representations? The final section of this chapter looks briefly at the relationship between media and events, and shows how this particular type of representation of space can influence the construction of event narratives.

Finally, chapter 7 focuses on approaches that are useful to help us understand the practices and experiential nature of events. In this chapter we consider the concept of *habitus*, the importance of the social body and aspects of gender. *Habitus* helps us to explore further the relationship between structure and agency introduced in chapter 2. We note that the socialisation processes we are subject to as part of our upbringing and our on-going engagement with the world influences who we are, which in turn shapes our tastes, choices and actions. This approach is useful in a consideration of events because it helps us to think more carefully about how these factors, which are not always or often consciously expressed, help us to understand the varying motives for participating in events. The use of the body is central to ideas of *habitus* and so we discuss the roles that the senses and embodiment have in constructing the experiential nature of events. Thus, what the body feels or senses and how it moves during an event serves to embody the experience of the event, it becomes part of who we are. Notwithstanding the centrality of embodiment we also draw attention to how the body and how it is represented can be understood as symbolic. For example, dressing up for a day at the races could be interpreted as signalling that, for the attendee, this is a special occasion. The last element that we discuss in this chapter is the social construct of gender. We highlight the way in which, historically, some events have for example used the stereotype of the domestic to appeal to women, and how certain events in the present day can still serve to position women as the object of a male gaze.

2

EVENTS AND SOCIETY

As we argue in chapter 1, events are firmly rooted in and inextricably linked to society. That is, events are both products of the social world and contribute to the making of the social world. We have noted that these things we label events are becoming increasingly important in society. The purpose of this chapter is to consider some of the key ideas and issues that help us to understand the connection between events and the social world. The aims of this chapter are to:

- explain what is meant by the term 'society';
- explain the role of the individual in society in terms of 'structure' and 'agency';
- identify different phases in the development of society and the role of events during the eras identified;
- introduce and explain some key concepts in the social sciences that underpin our understandings of the social world.

Society – The term 'society' is not easy to define because, unlike the study of things in the 'natural' world by, for example, chemists, physicists and biologists, we cannot see this thing we call society. We can, however, make some general observations: the majority of people live in a social group within a bounded geographical area and this social group can be called a society. Within a society people can identify with each other based on common ways of behaving and thinking that do not reflect personal and individual opinions and attributes. There are many debates in the social sciences about the relationship between the overarching thing we call society and the person as individual. This is where the terms 'structure' and 'agency' are useful. Theories in the social sciences are often characterised by how much emphasis they give to agency or structure, which leads to debates about which one of these elements is the most important in determining behaviour. Some theorists have tried to go beyond this debate by arguing that the

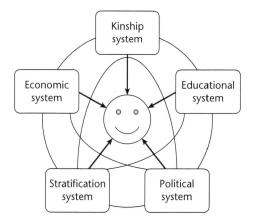

FIGURE 2.1 The relationship between the individual and social structures (adapted from Fulcher and Scott (2007))

subjective and objective are bound together and mutually informing (see, for example, the work of Pierre Bourdieu (1979); see also chapter 7 this volume).

Structure – 'Structure' refers to the system of interconnections between different aspects of society: for example, family and friendship groups and organisations based on religion, politics and economics, as well as other kinds of institutions including education and health care. If we are able to identify structures then we can also see how they can influence what we do. For example, we can recognise that some roles in society are associated with attributes associated with gender differences, and this in turn influences employment opportunities. Thus structure can be seen to be structuring. Figure 2.1 illustrates the relationship between structuring systems and the individual.

Agency – 'Agency' is a term often used in opposition to structure. Agency places emphasis on the individual and what she or he does. It is linked to notions of free will in that it includes ideas of choice and self-determination. In other words, an individual has the ability to act on her or his own, based on what she or he thinks.

An understanding of society can therefore come from how we as individuals behave within the overarching structure: in other words, how individuals interact

THINK POINT

In any given social context – a party, walking along the street, the village fête – there is the possibility that you will encounter people you do not know, people you vaguely know and people you know very well. How would you expect to react to these different groups of people and they to you? Consider words and acts of greeting and familiarity.

with other individuals and behave towards each other. Social interactions, which form the basis of the way that people behave towards each other, contribute to making the thing we call society.

In order to give the relationships we have meaning, we behave in certain ways. As the think point suggests, it could simply be through words of greeting, but it is also manifest in who we give presents to, who we eat and drink with, who we go out for entertainment with and so on. Society, then, is made up of different levels and forms of social interaction and relationships we engage in and create. Similarly, people rely on the structures of society to facilitate these relationships.

CASE STUDY: FESTIVE IDENTITY IN THE FIRE CARNIVAL OF THE FALLAS

In his study on personal and collective identity in the Fire Carnival of the Fallas of Valencia, Spain, Costa (2002) highlights the importance of sociability and, in particular, the communal sociability of the festival. The Fire Carnival is celebrated on the days leading up to St Joseph's day, with the climax being the burning of Las Fallas at midnight on 19 March. These artful wooden and paper sculptures – Las Fallas – are built by Falla associations throughout the year, with associations often being linked to different neighbourhoods in Valencia. Costa discusses the strong sociability that exists and is formed in the various festive associations and neighbourhoods. This sociability is characterised through the social interaction between people, the gathering of people from various backgrounds and its 'globalising and holistic quality'. 'Its festive sociability, anchored in a sense of street life, constitutes a good therapy against the effects of segmentation and isolation caused by modern life' (Costa 2002: 324). Young and old community members are encouraged to socialise as part of Las Fallas, with importance given to play (such as joke competitions), humour (verbal as well as presented through the sculptures), communal eating of dishes such as such as paella and bunyol, and sociable work in the preparation and building of Las Fallas.

(*Source*: Costa 2002)

How we behave towards others and the institutions we encounter is largely governed by our values, norms, roles and status. These things give structure to our behaviour, acting as guiding principles that help us to be organised in our response to the world. They form the basis for the way in which much of human behaviour is organised.

Roles – Every individual has a role in society. The role that one has can be related to employment, parenting, age and so on. For example, a woman can have roles as mother and financial adviser. A 10-year-old boy is both a son and a schoolchild. Each role is influenced and characterised by status, norms and values.

Values – Values refers to what we and society think is important. It is about what is understood to be right or wrong. For example we can hold the belief that everyone between the ages of 5 and 16 should go to school. Our understanding of why this is important and should be the case will be informed by how society treats the importance of universal education. Values will vary between individuals and societies.

Norms – Norms (short for 'normative' or 'normal') underpin our values and refer to what behaviour is expected in a given social situation. For example, when we first meet someone it may be normal for those of us based in western societies to shake hands. In other social groups it is the norm to bow. Some norms are legal and form laws which, if broken, lead to punishment. We have to learn norms and this leads us to ideas of the socialisation process, that is, where and when we learn the rules that govern our behaviour.

Status – Status refers to the social position used to define an individual's membership of society. For example, it could be related to hierarchy based on age in a family or an important public role. Inheriting the throne in the UK is at present based on being the eldest son.

Individual personalities, therefore, are shaped by the socialisation process – people are a product of their cultural upbringing. Our socialisation tells us such things as how to see the nature of the world and our position in that world. The relevance of having an understanding of these things as events students is that people's behaviours, norms, status and roles not only influence their decision to attend events, but also how they would behave at a specific event and, in turn, attendance at events can reinforce ideas of social roles. For example, the specific sporting activities which form part of the Olympics reflect changes in roles and status in society at a certain point in time, such as the recognition of women's boxing and snowboarding.

A classic text in social anthropology explores the relationship between the role of men in society and a particular event in Balinese village life. It is Clifford Geertz's (1973) analysis of cock-fighting. Geertz argues that the practice of cock-fighting is not simply about the contest between birds but is also a fight between the men who own the birds. He makes this claim based on the ways in which cocks are used as a metaphor for men in many aspects of Balinese society, stating 'court trials, wars, political contests, inheritance disputes, and street arguments are all compared to cockfights' (Geertz 1973: 418). As such, cock-fights represent aspects of Balinese society and the role of men in that society. According to Geertz (1973: 448), in practising the cock-fight the Balinese are in effect holding a mirror up to themselves and the fight becomes a story: '[i]ts function is interpretive: it is a Balinese reading of Balinese experience, a story they tell themselves about themselves'. Thus, this 'focussed gathering' (Geertz 1973: 424) is a display or performance of a narrative which makes up Balinese society.

From this we can think about the tension between ourselves as individuals and the institutions that we relate to and interact with and how these, in turn, influence our behaviour. For example, think about crowd-control measures enforced at sporting events, music events, film premiers and large-scale public celebrations, for example Queen Elizabeth's Jubilee events in 1977, 2002 and 2012. This demonstrates that we cannot necessarily always do what we would like and therefore in situations like this we lack agency (we will pick up on this point again in chapter 4).

A discussion of the social significance of events and the role of events within society leads to an analysis of the development of such occurrences over time. When considering this, the link between thought, action and social organisation at a certain point in time directly influences and is influenced by the economic, political and cultural concepts of a certain era. This is reflected in different forms of and rationales for public events, festivals and other types of celebrations over past centuries, which were directed by society's norms, values and roles at the time. We can identify two distinct phases of societies' development, the pre-modern and the modern. We begin with the pre-modern, with its main focus on political and religious events.

Pre-modern society

During pre-modern times the economic organisation of society was dominated by relatively simple divisions of labour in terms of labourer versus landowner, soldier versus general/officer and the inflexibility of the class system. It was pre-industrial, so society was based mainly on agriculture, with land ownership linked to power. During this period each individual and group within society had an ascribed status and role, which they were expected to conform to. From a political perspective, pre-modern society was a totalitarian system, where the state shared power with the Church and controlled society's norms, values and roles. This is not unlike ideas attached to totalitarianism associated with some modern political systems. It was patriarchal, and the country was ruled by a minority, underlined by a very rigid system of social stratification. In other words, an individual's ascribed social and economic status defined their role within society where men had the dominant roles. In general, the Church dominated society through a powerful and unchallenged religious belief system, with the idea of the divine right of kings theory giving monarchs the right to rule directly from God.

Events during this period reflect these conditions. On the one hand, festivals were supposed to make society celebrate and admire the political authority, and thus ensure continued order and control, while religion invoked celebrations such as saints' days and other religious holidays. In addition, the political and religious struggles that mark this era found expression in the events of wars and related activities.

THINK POINT

Pre-modern festivals and events were dominated by a patriarchal political system, peasant beliefs and the status of religion. How has this changed since then? What role do politics and religion play in today's events?

The development of communal festive customs slowly emerged through religious gatherings and wakes in some parish communities in England but subsequently declined due to political and religious factors in the form of increasing attempts to examine, control and eventually legislate to stop the practice of wakes (Hutton 1994, cited in Hindle 1995: 156). As Hindle (1995: 156) explains 'Wakes were subjected to increasingly close official scrutiny as part of a wider process of moral regulation in late sixteenth- and early seventeenth-century England.' This illustrates the close link between political and religious dominance of societal norms and values, and their influence on festive customs and cultures.

CASE STUDY: EUROPEAN MEDIEVAL HOLIDAYS AND FESTIVALS

Monthly secular and religious events are discussed in Cosman's (1984) book, which explores different medieval holidays and festivals throughout the year, with particularly important celebrations being held throughout winter and spring. Below is a summary of some of the holidays and festivals described by Cosman:

January: Twelfth Night

This festivity refers to the celebration of the 12 days of Christmas, with the conclusion and largest celebration taking place on the twelfth day, 5 January. Traditional entertainment and customs include wearing disguises, for example people wearing antlers and bells on their shoes, which was complemented by the Guise Procession, during which people performed gestures according to their disguise. Two cakes were baked (the Twelfth Cake), one for women and one for men, in which a bean for men and a pea for women were hidden. Whoever found the pea and bean were crowned the King and Queen of the Bean and were allowed to sit at the high table. Many other traditions and rituals formed part of the celebrations such as 'Wassailing the Trees', fires held outside, 'Oxhorn cake and the Oxhorn Dance', 'The Hobby Horse', a Mummers' Play and a re-enactment of the biblical story of the Three Kings' Star.

February: St Valentine's Day

This festival of love involved many love-related decorations and games, though the origins of the festival and who St Valentine was are unknown. Love lanterns and fragrant decorations were spread around halls, guests to the celebrations wore love tokens, such as love-knot jewellery, love sleeves and hearts sewn to garments while music called the *chivaree* was played. Food played an important role, with some dishes that were known to 'stimulate affection' and others known to 'quiet emotions'. Pairing games were played during the celebrations and conversations were meant to focus on love.

April: All Fools' Day

This festival took place to remind people that disorder can ultimately be disastrous and rules exist for reason. 'The April world is upside down. Things are not what they seem. Elegant order is turned topsy-turvy. The results are hilarious. All Fool's Day is a splendid celebration of the ridiculous' (Cosman 1984: 48). Thus, festivities included a guest becoming 'The Lord of Misrule, Motley, and Whiddershins', boys playing bishops and the young ruling the old. In addition, feasts are held such as the Feast of Fools. And this takes us back to the terminology identified in chapter 1 and the idea of carnival and the carnivalesque.

October: Halloween

The end of October is the end of the year in the ancient pagan Celtic calendar and the beginning of Winter. It is a festival of spirits and is closely linked to the religious day of All Hallows or All Saints' Day, which is celebrated on the next day. As such Halloween presents a mix of pagan and religious celebrations. Similar to other festivals mentioned above, specific food, role plays and theatrical performances characterised this holiday in medieval times. Thus, a guest played the role of a ruler, in this case King Crispin; games and entertainments included 'Hunt the Slipper' and the play of St George and Crowdie; and a dish of sweet cream mixed with apple sauce is consumed.

(*Source*: Cosman 1984)

Having considered the pre-modern we have to understand some of the changes that led to modern society.

Modern society

There is no specific date to the beginning or end of modern society but what we can identify are changes that impacted social organisation and social relations and make the social world distinctly different from that of pre-modern times. These changes can also be seen in relation to event practices. The forces of modernity are on-going and have developed to such an extent that, as we will see later, some have identified a third era of societal development in the form of the postmodern. However, for now we are using the term 'modern' to include the time from around the start of industrialisation to the present.

One of the greatest changes to pre-modern society was in economic organisation with the beginnings of industrialisation. Mass production, the idea of Fordism (industrial mass production) and Taylorism (the analysis and management of work flow) developed and were pushed during this era so that they influenced and dominated socio-economic advances. There was an increased use of money and capitalist economies developed. With this increase in a division of labour, democracy developed and absolute power declined. Thus, the status of individuals was not so rigidly ascribed and they were able to move between classes. A wide spectrum of festivals developed so that a distinct event-related culture during the early times of the modern era emerged. Mosse (1971: 172) notes: 'Festivals to be given at regular intervals were designed in part to overcome class differences, for people would take part in them regardless of social status.' Nevertheless, specific events existed to strengthen people's loyalty to monarchs and political authority, and religious and political events still sustained this. However, in addition, events with different political purposes emerged. For example, the French Revolution in 1789 led to a collapse of the absolute monarchy in France and was succeeded by a period called the Bourbon Restoration, which saw many festivals with political purposes. However, rather than advocating people's allegiance to a monarch they were celebrating the new nationalism and became 'instruments of popular democracy' (Bonet-Maury 1896, cited in Mosse 1971: 171), with the first national day celebrations taking place in Strasbourg on 14 July 1880. This has now become Bastille day, which is the French National Day, and is still celebrated on the 14 July each year.

During this time types of public events expanded and the number of events increased, with communal celebrations emerging in particular. Identifying a community can be complex because it is not always easy to see where the boundaries – both physical and symbolic – are situated. We can understand a community as a group of individuals acting/functioning as a social network that can 'provide identity, meaning and a sense of self-worth to their members' (Milne 1998: 40). Thus, each community will have its individual characteristics and is not necessarily spatially bound. Aligning this to the context of an increase in communal celebrations, Tenfelde (1978) discusses the development of a distinct festive culture during this era by providing a detailed analysis of festivals in mining communities in the nineteenth century. In this case, the sense of self-worth of the community stems from a shared occupation. Links can be drawn from Tenfelde's discussion of mining communities to other occupations. Thus, many communal festivals and celebrations during this time derived from customs which grew out of laws and occupational advancement, for example the granting of fiefdoms. Other celebrations built on customs of occupational associations such as fraternities, and on customs of communal and religious festivals like the sharing of wedding celebrations. Political and religious events still occurred regularly but were of course influenced by the economic, political and cultural concepts of the era and each country, such as ritual acknowledgements of political authority and communal religious events like Thanksgiving.

Moving to the twentieth century, we can identify a different pattern of changes that influenced the practice of events. In the introduction we referred to the

FIGURE 2.2 Saltney Christmas parade, 2009
Source: © Les Roberts.

increasing number of events in recent years. Jeremy Boissevain (1992) has noted that in Europe the number of public celebrations is expanding. He quotes Frank Manning (1983: 4, in Boissevain 1992: 1), who claims that: 'throughout both the industrialized and developing nations, new celebrations are being created and older ones revived on a scale that is surely unmatched in human history'. For example, in 2009 the north Wales town of Saltney held its first community Christmas celebrations, beginning with a parade along the main street involving local schoolchildren, youth groups and residents (see Figure 2.2). The parade ended at the centre of town where the crowd were entertained by choirs from local schools and other attractions.

The explanation given for the increased number of public celebrations is explored by Boissevain (1992) in relation to some of the conditions that are said to characterise the modern era. First he notes that immediately following the Second World War public celebrations went into decline. He attributes this to the following factors:

1   Massive migration from areas of southern Europe to northern Europe by people in search of work. This meant that there were simply not enough people to continue with the organisation and practice of festivals in the rural communities that they had left behind.
2   The processes and practices of industrialisation made the traditional functional use of rituals to mark time and phases of the agricultural cycle less important.
3   Increased secularisation as the role of the Church diminishes in importance in everyday life which makes the religious basis of events less significant.

As the features of modernity have become more entrenched leading to an era of advanced modernity, reactions to social conditions also developed and changed. As Boissevain (1992) contends, no one thing can account for the renewed interest in events but we can look at some of the developments and attitudes to modernity that can be argued to have triggered an increase in events from around the 1970s onwards. These are:

1   Migration from southern Europe slowed and in some cases reversed. The practice of visiting friends and relatives 'at home' often occurred at the same time as key community celebrations, for example Christmas and Easter, giving such activities renewed focus.
2   Industrialisation is associated with increased urbanisation and, for many, unsatisfactory living and working conditions, which leads to questioning of the underpinning values and ethos of modernity. According to Boissevain (1992: 8) 'this in turn has led to a revalorization of "traditional", often rural, life-styles, including the rituals associated with them'. We will return to the important role that the ideals and ideas attached to rural life have for events later in the chapter.
3   Although for many the forces of modernity gave rise to improved living standards, the associated feelings of anomie and isolation have also led to seeking out more community celebrations.
4   The rise of media: the increased dissemination of information in various forms of media 'stimulated the rapid dissemination of ritual practices' (Boissevain 1992: 9) which in turn caused people to reflect on their own celebrations.
5   The development of mass tourism: following the Second World War the ability of people to travel for leisure and pleasure purposes increased. As part of this process visitors in search of something different became increasingly interested in the festivals, rituals and celebrations that they encountered during their touristic practices.
6   Democratisation: the end of dictatorships in parts of Europe (for example the death of Franco in 1975, the end of the military junta in Greece in 1974, the success of the Labour Party in Malta in 1971 and the fall of the Eastern bloc) meant that activities that had long been suppressed found new outlets and importance. The case study 'Public celebrations in a Spanish valley' illustrates some of the points raised above.

CASE STUDY: PUBLIC CELEBRATIONS IN A SPANISH VALLEY

This case study is based on pilgrimages, rituals and festivities found in the Jerte Valley, in northern Extremadura in western Spain. A number of saints' days and religious celebrations are found in the different villages. Cruces and Díaz de Rada make a number of observations about the changes in the celebrations that illustrate the 'evolution' of the festivities in part in relation to forces of modernisation.

The first observation is that a number of events has gone into decline. For example, at the village of Navaconcejo villagers no longer make the pilgrimage up the mountain but instead stay in or near to the village. Only three villages in the Jerte Valley continue to celebrate Holy Cross Day and no one now celebrates the festivals of St John and St Peter. These and similar activities that have also gone into decline in the area are linked to the religious calendar. Processes of modernisation have meant that the agricultural production of the village communities has become specialised and it is this new agricultural cycle that caused the downturn in the religious festivities. In addition the increased secularisation of society has meant that the importance attached to religious celebrations has greatly reduced.

The second observation is related to celebrations that have continued and been 'revitalised' following the slowdown in emigration from the valley. These festivities include the patronal feasts of villages, which coincide with the return of emigrants for their summer holidays. These celebrations mix traditional and recently introduced elements 'which relate to the process of modernization of the area' (Cruces and Díaz de Rada 1992: 66). The festivities no longer reflect just the agricultural or religious calendar but, because of the link for some of the events to the return to the valley of villagers' family members (e.g. children and grandchildren) the cycle of rituals reflects 'urban holidays'.

A third observation is connected to the development of communication, such as the televising of some rituals. This feature has increased interest in the festivities from outside the valley and also impacted on their performance. For example, the pageant of St Sebastian in Piornal was delayed due to the presence of cameras impeding the movement of one of the key ritual characters.

A fourth observation relates to the changes in the practice of the celebrations. For example the rules relating to bullfights. The traditional method is to rope the bull by the horns whereas a newer development is to use the services of a professional bullfighter. In other instances, while celebrations retain a core liturgical element often the celebrations 'overflow' to the days either side of the actual saint's day and involve dancing in discotheques. Such activities are not organised by the church.

(*Source*: Cruces and Díaz de Rada 1992)

Fournier (2007) also identified another facet behind the rise in festivals which refers to the valorisation of culture. Culture is a notoriously slippery concept but it can be understood as the practices and performances of a group of people which in turn can lead to cultural productions. For example if a group of people share the same cooking habits and use a certain type of bowl to mix their food we can say that they share a cultural practice of cooking. They may make the bowl and that bowl conforms to a certain standard of shape and dimensions. The bowl is a cultural production and forms a part of material culture (those things that we can touch, hold and smell). Material culture often forms the basis of tourists' souvenirs. Other forms of cultural expression are manifest in dance, theatre and ritual. These are also cultural productions but are examples of non-material culture in that they cannot be touched only viewed. Although we cannot touch a dance or celebration they can still be packaged and sold. Events are often used to 'showcase' a particular place and are often another feature of tourism marketing strategies. In this way they become commodities. We will return to the theme of commodification and consumption practices in chapter 5 but for now it is enough to note that the recognition of the possibilities of commercial exploitation attached to events has – as Fournier (2007: 4) notes – meant that 'they have become new social and economic resources'.

This is particularly so if we acknowledge the economy as a dynamic, sociospatial, and differentiated economic landscape embedded in place-specific cultural contexts and social relations; here we become aware of a shift towards an awareness but also a research agenda embracing the cultural dimensions of the economy, politics and emphasising agency and social relations (Mosedale 2011). Political forces are crucial in determining economic outputs and there seems to be a trend to use events in a similar way to that which Britton (1991: 465) identified for tourism in that it is a 'capitalistically organised activity driven by the inherent and defining social dynamics of that system, with its attendant production, social and ideological relations'. The case study 'Capital of Culture' illustrates this point.

CASE STUDY: EUROPEAN CAPITAL OF CULTURE

In 1985 the European Union launched a cultural initiative called the European Capital of Culture with the aim of providing education about cultural diversity, recognising ethnic diversity within the unity of the European project and providing opportunities to experience the diverse scope of European cultures. It is underpinned by the notion of bonding through cultural awareness, and efforts to change the face and character and economic base of a city. As such, it was the first large-scale collaborative cultural project and has since taken place annually. The first European Capital of Culture was Athens in 1985, followed by one European city each year until the millennium when nine cities were elected: Avignon (France), Bergen (Norway), Bologna (Italy), Brussels (Belgium), Helsinki (Finland), Cracow (Poland), Prague (Czech Republic), Reykjavík (Iceland) and Santiago de Compostela (Spain). Since then there have been one to three European Capitals of Culture each year. Cities' commitment in terms of economic investment and other resource investments is substantial, so key benefits to the cities are not only considered to take the form of cultural development but also economic development and long-term rejuvenation/

revitalisation. On the one hand, cities take part to showcase and celebrate their culture over a whole year, and thus develop pride in the local culture and potentially encourage a sense of European identity. On the other hand, the Capital of Culture status and the subsequent economic and financial contribution needed to revitalise cities are considered key to encouraging long-term development and revitalisation of the cities and to redefining its image as a place to live in. The status helps to put cities back on the tourist map as illustrated in the following statement:

> After 25 years of European Capitals of Culture, their urban, touristic and economic potential and the role they play towards promoting social cohesion is undeniable. They offer a unique opportunity for urban regeneration and image boosting both at a European and an international level.
>
> *(European Commission 2009: 10)*

For example

> Glasgow 1990 is deemed to have rejuvenated a city suffering from urban decay, heavy unemployment and a reputation for street crime, with many positive after-effects on the creative scene and a radical boost to its international image. Not only do cafés fill its streets on sunny days, but it is now considered a major cultural tourism destination.
>
> *(European Commission 2009: 5)*

The main challenge for many cities is to balance the political support, the economic investment and the artistic and cultural freedom. Links between city and civic organisations and the relationship between city and region are key for this rejuvenation.

(*Source*: European Commission 2009)

In many respects we see that the reactions to modernity that Boissevain (1992) identifies have led to a focus on a rural ideal. Indeed, if we were to look at the numerous property programmes broadcast on UK television we would find that many of them involve a desire to escape from a large urban area to what is seen as a more cosy, peaceful and less stressful life in a rural setting. The reality of such imagined geographies is of course open to debate. What we would note is that the interest in all things rural and natural, from home location to baking one's own brown bread, is echoed in the field of events by the increasing number of events that are set in rural locations or have some idea of the rural/natural at their heart.

For example Lawton and Weaver (2010) note that birding festivals (the watching of and interaction with wild birds) have undergone a dramatic increase in North

America in the past 12 or so years. In the early 1990s there were 10–15 such events, by 2006 there were 200, with over 71 million Americans participating in some kind of wildlife watching and spending in excess of USD45 billion. Lawton and Weaver argue that the rise is part of a trend towards more nature-based forms of consumption practice. A key feature of the birding festival experience is that it should offer a contrast to urban environments. Janiskee (1980) also recognises the urge of urban day-trippers to attend rural festivals to experience agricultural practices. His case study of rural South Carolina's Harvest Festivals highlights urbanites' attraction to harvest festivals because of 'their ready accessibility, novelty and emphasis on something-for-everybody family fun with a distinctive "down home country flavor"' (Janiskee 1980: 96). A study regarding the development of rural festivals in southern New Zealand highlights the increased demand in festivals and events in rural settings, with the focus shifting away from traditional agricultural practices to a greater focus on events linked to produce, such as the Bluff Oyster/Seafood Festival, and sporting activities, such as the Kepler Challenge in Fiordland National Park (Higham and Ritchie 2001). Table 2.1 represents a chronological development of rural events in southern New Zealand and illustrates the change in event characteristics and goals over the years.

The point here is that ideas of the countryside – often associated with nature and 'tradition' in terms of practices and produce and therefore linked to the pre-modern world – are becoming increasingly significant, and contributing to renewed interest in rural-based festivals (see for example Gibson *et al.* 2011). They appeal to the modern consumer by offering experiences away from the urban environment while also increasing a more diversified rural economy. This development is reflected in Pine and Gilmore's (1998) notion of an experience economy, in that modern consumers are now looking for unique, personal and memorable experiences; this will be further explored in chapter 5.

THINK POINT

Think about the last time you were at a rural event/festival. How were the local community and local traditions represented?

Handelman (1998) claims that public events serve to *present* (mirror) existing social order directly, *re-present* it more indirectly, and/or *model* socio-cultural realities in a way that may imply change. Thus, how the various ideals of modernity – which have been discussed in our section on modern society – have influenced the development of events can be illustrated by looking at the modern Olympics. Based on the ideals of modernity, the Olympics were officially re-established for largely political reasons in 1896, namely as a means to advocate 'the reconciliation of warring nations' (Guttmann 2002: 1). Nevertheless, the Olympics movement has

TABLE 2.1 Chronological classification of rural events based on the year of initiation (adapted from Higham and Ritchie (2001: 45))

Era/events	Event characteristics	Event/festival goal
1863–1969 A and P Shows NZ Merino Shearing Champs Alexandra Blossom Festival	• Integrated into traditional rural lifestyles • Survived the 'test of time'	• Child and adult entertainment • Sale of crafts • Promotion of agriculture • Celebration of seasons • Community fundraising
1970–87 Spring Exhibition Hokonui Fashion Queenstown Winter Festival Glenorchy Races Carnival Glenorchy Fishing Competition Festival of Visual Performing Arts Golden Guitars Southern Field Days Cromwell Fruit Carnival	• Linked to traditional rural events, activities and interests • Diversification from traditional rural lifestyles (e.g. exhibitions) • Portrayal of rich and diverse rural living • First tourism-specific event (Queenstown Winter Festival)	• Promote art and talent • Society club interests and community fundraising • Tourism and regional economic development
1988–98 St Bathans' Ghost to Ghost Millbrook Concert Bluff Oyster/Seafood Festival Bannockburn Mountainbike Queenstown Food and Jazz Omarama Gliding Championship Maniototo Winter Festival Otago Gold Heritage Trust Cavalcade Gala Day Rhododendron Festival Goldrush Days Southern Traverse Tuatapere Challenge Blues, Brews and Barbeques Warbirds over Wanaka Kepler Challenge Hokonui Music Festival	• Distinctive and innovative events and festivals • Dependent upon non-local participation for success • Rise of sporting events • Pursuit of synergies with local geographic and historic resources	• Fundraising • Civic pride • Image creation • Promotion • Tourism attraction development • Regional economic development • Countering tourism seasonality • Using recreational facilities during off-season • Heritage protection • Holiday entertainment • Media attention

always claimed to be apolitical (Klausen 1999a) and free of religious constraints. Since then the Olympics have been presented as being free of religious associations, the only faith being 'good sportsmanship and fair play' (Guttmann 2002: 3), which reflects the modern drive towards secularisation in that religion is seen as being less important than during pre-modern times. Thus, the Olympic Games express and legitimise values of modernity: 'the Olympic motto "Citius, Altius, Fortius" [swifter, higher, stronger] is a condensed expression of the values inherent in the creative and innovative endeavours, characteristic of everything that is modern in manufacture, science, art and self-realisation' (Klausen 1999c: 5). The Games serve a broad spectrum of interests and the concept of a global village, in the form of universality and global homogenisation, is embedded in the Olympic Games. This makes them polysemous (they express multiple meanings) and thus supportive of some of the characteristics – pluralism and relativism – associated with modernity. In 1994 Norway wanted to use the 1994 Winter Games to display the country's status as a modern entity. However, the opening ceremony was replete with references more associated with the pre-modern world, to the extent that Klausen (1999a: 44) referred to 'an orgy of folkloric elements'. This divide between 'traditional' and modern was reflected throughout the Games, as ultimately the Olympic movement is in the vanguard of modernism (Klausen 1999a) while at the same time national customs and ideas were used to represent ideas of 'Norwegianness'.

We have noted how the forces of modernity brought about a change in people's living conditions compared to pre-modern times. Table 2.2 summarises the major characteristics of each era. It also makes links to two theories in the social sciences which seek to make sense of the changes and how they inform social relations and interactions.

Tönnies was concerned with modernisation processes in Europe, which he argued were characterised by a passage from relations based on community to those based on rationality and calculation. The idea being that the community relations were with people with whom one had an emotional connection – family and friends or working group – and who were connected to a particular place, for example a village: this is referred to as *Gemeinschaft*. The word *Gesellschaft* is linked to the development of urban areas and the rationalisation processes associated with industrialisation. People are both more socially and more physically mobile (that is, people no longer have to accept their prescribed status in life and will journey on from the place in which they were born). Societies which can be considered as *Gesellschaft* have the characteristics of heterogeneity and impersonality, in which the individual is left more to their own devices than in the world of *Gemeinschaft*.

Durkheim's idea of mechanical and organic solidarity is similar. In the world of mechanical solidarity social networks are small and based on close relations within family or clan groups. Individualism is low and people perform work tasks together, with no or only a little specialisation. There is little self-determination, and custom and obligation play important roles in creating social cohesion. In this type of society religion has a dominant part to play in creating actions and dispositions and deviance is dealt with by a repressive penal system. With the onset of industrialisation and urbanisation, bigger population groups spread over a larger geographical area. This was accompanied by the rise of the individual, in which one person is linked to another through contractual rather than emotional obligations. The division of labour is more complex, as specific roles are performed by specific people through specialisation of tasks. Individuals also have rights prescribed in law, and the penal system seeks to redress wrongdoing through the judicial system. This system is restorative in that, in most cases, individuals return to society following punishment rather than being executed or deported and therefore totally excluded. What both Tönnies' and Durkheim's theories tell us is that the social world and the way people behave towards each other has changed, and that perhaps in this change something has been lost – for example a sense of moral obligation towards other people.

TABLE 2.2 Pre-modern versus modern society

	Pre-modern	*Modern*
Economic	Simple division of labour Pre-industrial Subsistence Agriculture	Industrial Mass production Complex division of labour Capitalist Fordist
Political	State and Church dominated Feudal Social mobility Closed fragmentation – no nation state	Democracy Decline in absolute monarchy Rise in nation state
Cultural	Religion dominates tradition	Reason and progress Science Experimental Objectivity
Pace of change	Slow change and development	Fast change and development
Theory	Tönnies: *Gemeinschaft* Durkheim: Mechanical solidarity	Tönnies: *Gesellschaft* Durkheim: Organic solidarity
Emotional ties/ Social cohesion	Close, face to face; known 'in-group'; strong cohesion	Impersonality; lack of emotional bonding; links by contract
Division of labour	Low	High
Place	Attachment	Mobile
Individual	Ascribed social status Low individualism	Personality Rise of individual
Penal/judicial system	Repressive, violent and swift	Restorative
Religion	Dominant	Less significant

The theories we have identified are those explored by Emile Durkheim in the form of mechanical and organic solidarity and Ferdinand Tönnies in relation to the worlds of *Gemeinschaft* and *Gesellschaft*. What both approaches identify is the idea that the processes of modernisation, with their attendant industrialisation and urbanisation, have led to something being lost to humankind. This loss relates to ideas of naturalness and is strongly associated with smaller rural communities.

The preceding section has been framed by the term 'the modern'. As we have previously said, these eras are not fixed in date but are understood in relation to processes such as technological advances, which impact upon social structures and relations. The latter half of the twentieth century has also seen rapid developments in the world wide web and use of internet, which have changed the way people relate to each other through new ways of communication, in parallel with an increasingly mobile society. At the same time, our understandings of knowledge creation have been challenged to recognise plurality in social existence (for example, recognising different perspectives such as feminism and postcolonialism), which has led some people to identify a new era called the postmodern. This is the subject of the next section.

Postmodern society

It is hard to put a date on postmodernity and the jury is out on whether it is a 'new' era or not, so boundaries between the modern and postmodern are considered blurred. Postmodernism is recognised as a direct reaction to modernity. The idea of one truth and one reality is questioned and society is considered as being different from before, largely due to the continued processes of globalisation and the increased movement of people. The postmodern society is seen as being dominated by transnational companies, advanced capitalism, trading blocs and common policies, the introduction of the web and rapid development of new technologies. The features of postmodernity relate to post-Fordism (related to ideas of a multi-skilled and flexible workforce), individualisation, the importance of the consumer, for example the focus on niche markets (such as specialised festivals like historical re-enactments) and the decline of the nation state. In pre-modern social organisation the structure of societies is limited, given the smaller number of roles that people are expected to perform. In the modern or postmodern eras the situation is more complex as there is a huge range of possibilities and therefore a greater number of social roles. The event context is not outside these global frameworks and developments, as MacLeod (2006: 235) argues:

> The processes that have contributed to a disarticulation between ideas of identity and place have produced an approach to festival development and promotion that increasingly depends for its appeal on a new type of transnationalised festivity rather than local meanings, traditions and social practice. These processes can be approached through the globalisation of communications networks and the expanding international tourism market.

In this context, communities and community festivals are no longer considered as unique and interesting emanations of local culture but as opportunities for convivial consumption in an international 'placeless' atmosphere. . . [F]estival formats may now be replicated in a series of international venues throughout the world.

The Oktoberfest, which is traditionally celebrated in Munich in September and October, had its beginnings with the marriage between Crown Prince Ludwig and Princess Therese von Sachsen-Hildburghausen in 1810. Nowadays, the concept of the Oktoberfest has spread to different nations, with a focus on the consumption and celebration of beer rather than an awareness and celebration of Bavarian customs and rituals, which still form important elements of the Munich Oktoberfest. Having removed the link to 'place', Oktoberfests can now be found around the globe from Yokohama, Japan, to Big Bear in California.

THINK POINT

Think about a top European football club. Where do the players come from and who makes up their fan base? How can this be linked to the idea of the postmodern?

From the example of football we can see how national boundaries are being crossed for work and leisure. This links to the idea that identities are no longer as fixed as they once were, but rather are more fluid and changeable. Football teams are no longer composed of 'home-grown' players and fans are not purely local. A characteristic of postmodernity is being able to play with identity. If we consider the popular cultural icons of Madonna and Lady Gaga we can see how, for reasons associated with play, parody, irony and a desire to challenge established cultural norms – often related to gendered or sexualised identities – they adopt different personas and guises in their performances.

Ideas of irony and playfulness and challenges to conventional understandings of identities can be seen in the annual event of the Eurovision Song Contest. Established in 1956, the competition was initiated to identify the 'best' song in Europe and its winning was associated with ideas of national identity and pride. The contest has since developed and involves more ironic and comedic acts. In this respect, controversial performers such as Israel's transsexual Dana International (the winner in 1998) and Germany's Guildo Horn have been seen to undermine the seriousness of the event.

The song contest is broadcast live on international television. This brings us to another central aspect of the postmodern world: the importance of media not only in producing ever-changing images for us to engage with; but also offering environments in which we can play with our own identities, for example virtual worlds. We will pick up these themes again in later chapters.

Summary

In this chapter we have:

- explored the evolution of society in terms of the pre-modern, modern and postmodern worlds;
- introduced theories developed by Tönnies and Durkheim to help us to understand the different characteristics of the pre-modern and modern worlds;
- introduced ideas and terminology that help us to understand the relationship between the individual and society;
- identified changes in society that have impacted on the rise and fall of events and the increased interest in rural events.

Suggested reading

Boissevain, J. (1992) *Revitalizing European Rituals*. London: Routledge.
Costa, X. (2002) 'Festive Identity: Personal and Collective Identity in the Fire Carnival of the "Fallas" (Valencia, Spain)', *Social Identities: Journal for the Study of Race, Nation and Culture*, 8(2): 321–45.
Fulcher, J. and Scott, J. (2007) *Sociology*. Oxford: Oxford University Press.
Geertz, C. (1973) *The Interpretation of Cultures*. New York: Basic Books.
Gibson, C., Connell, J., Waitt, G. and Walmsley, J. (2011) 'The Extent and Significance of Rural Festivals', in C. Gibson and J. Connell (eds) (2011) *Festival Places: Revitalising Rural Australia*. Bristol: Channel View, 3–24.
Lloyd, F. (1993) *Deconstructing Madonna*. London: Batsford.
MacLeod, N.E. (2006) 'The Placeless Festival: Identity and Place in the Post-modern Festival', in D. Picard and M. Robinson (eds) *Festivals, Tourism and Social Change*. Clevedon: Channel View Publications.

Useful websites

International Olympic Committee: http://www.olympic.org
Carnivals in Las Fallas: http://www.valenciavalencia.com/culture-guide/fallas/carnivals-fallas.htm
European Commission – Culture: http://ec.europa.eu/culture/our-programmes-and-actions/capitals/european-capitals-of-culture_en.htm
St Patrick's Day Festival: http://www.stpatricksfestival.ie
Oktoberfest: http://www.oktoberfest.de/en
Eurovision Song Contest: http://www.eurovision.tv

3

EVENTS AND RITUAL

As we have seen in chapter 2, many events have a cyclical nature, by which we mean that they are practised on a regular basis and often at the same time of each calendar year (see for example the case study detailing medieval holidays and festivals, p. 14). This means that these types of activities are repeated actions and they can therefore be understood as rituals.

The purpose of this chapter is to explore some of the key ideas relating to rituals and to examine how we can understand events in these terms. The aims of this chapter are to:

- understand what rituals are;
- understand rites of passage;
- understand secular rituals;
- explore the idea of invented tradition and its relationship to events.

Ritual

Ritual refers to any form of repeated action that takes place at a regular and set time. If we take this definition then many aspects of a our daily lives could be understood as ritual, for example every time we clean our teeth before bed, if we always have a cup of tea when we get home from university or work. If we were to leave our understanding of ritual there it would render the term quite meaningless because so many of our daily activities rely on a known, habitual way of doing things. To understand more clearly the significance of ritual we need to look more carefully at the social significance of the behaviours, attitudes and beliefs attached to rituals. To explore this in more detail we can think about the example in the case study 'Between inside and outside'.

CASE STUDY: BETWEEN INSIDE AND OUTSIDE

In Japan everyone removes their shoes before they enter someone else's or their own house. Removing the shoes emphasises the difference between the two different types of spaces – inside the house and outside the house. The latter is considered dirty and even dogs have to have their paws wiped before they are let inside. The removal of shoes and the cleaning of dogs' paws takes place in the porch or at the gate of the property. These spaces are neither inside nor outside but are in-between spaces across which the movement between inside and outside takes place. As transitional zones, the porch or gate areas are ambiguous and associated with danger. Thus they are treated in a different way from the clearly defined inside and outside and subject to daily cleaning. Their crossing is also linked to special words of greeting and goodbye. In addition on returning home people may change their clothes and wash, which again marks the difference between the inside and outside. These activities are so firmly ingrained in Japanese society that we say that they are rituals.

(*Source*: Ozaki and Lewis 2006)

In the example of Japanese practices around entering and exiting the house attention is drawn to the way that we categorise the social world. It is often the case that we draw distinctions based on opposites for example day/night, black/white, in/out but not everything fits neatly into a category; there are states and places in between, for example twilight and the colour grey. The porch is a place between the inside and the outside. As we move between the different neat categories that we identify, when things are not quite one thing or another we are perhaps uncertain and feel a sense of danger. In order to defend ourselves against this danger we perform certain practices that help us guard against the perceived threat. People's practices, or the things they do in response to perceived danger often become rituals. Therefore we can understand ritual as prescribed behaviour that we do not really question. Breaking the norms of a particular practice will confirm if it is ritual or not, because if no one responds then no expected code of behaviour has been breached. Thus, the ritual values that are attached to certain ways of acting would not have been broken.

At this point we would also like to note that danger can become the focus of the celebrations associated with some events. Indeed, Datta (1993) discusses the *Fête de la Vache Enragée* in the Montmartre district of Paris, France, organised in 1896 and 1897 by the artist Adolphe Willette and other Montmartre-based Bohemians. The festival was a parody of the 'official' *Fête du Boeuf Gras* – which celebrated plenty – and sought to highlight the difficulties of the poor in the Montmartre district. As such 'for Montmartre residents, artists and others [it] was an emblem of Montmartre life; it evoked the ever present dangers they faced, hunger and poverty' (Datta 1993: 199). At the same time the festival served to demonstrate opposition to the Catholic Church and an increasing role on the part of the national government to control festivals. For example, the organisers of the *Vache Enragée* saw civic festivals organised by the government (such as Bastille Day) as bourgeois. The *Vache Enragée* was an attempt to create a festival that was independent of the strictures and ideologies associated with the government.

THINK POINT

What things do you celebrate in life? What form do the celebrations take? How do you think you would feel if things that are normally part of your celebrations were left out or changed?

Reflecting on discussions regarding the term 'event' and aligning these with the idea of rituals emphasises the importance of having an understanding of what a ritual is and its wider meaning for event management students. Thus, Falassi (1987: 2) defined festivals as:

> a periodically recurrent, social occasion in which, through a multiplicity of forms and a series of coordinated events, participate directly or indirectly and to various degrees, all members of a whole community, united by ethnic, linguistic, religious, historical bonds, and sharing a world view.

The key elements of a ritual namely, recurrence, special occasion and the time element are clearly reflected in this definition. An example for a ritual is shown in Figure 3.1, in which the Duke of Northumberland throws a football from Alnwick castle to the waiting crowd below. This ritual forms part of the Shrove Tuesday celebrations and represents the beginning of the annual football game, which then takes place on the pastures by the river Aln.

Other event literature focuses more on the managerial link between rituals and events. Brown and James (2004: 53) suggest that contemporary event management has sacrificed any ritualistic elements 'in favour of artificially manufacturing events', while also questioning whether the need and hurry to create an event industry has led to sacrificing an awareness of rituals in the event context. While we echo these arguments, Brown and James's (2004) discussion largely focuses on elements of event design and event management rather than an actual discussion of issues relating to the socio-cultural practices of rituals.

Rituals can be classified into different types, with the most profound being rites of passage, discussed further below. The various types of rites are categorised according to their key characteristics, such as their symbolic meanings, myths, transformation and consumption elements, all of which can be linked to the event context.

FIGURE 3.1 Shrove Tuesday ritual at Alnwick

Source: © Teresa Leopold.

THINK POINT

Reflecting back on the celebrations that you identified, have a look at Table 3.1 and attempt to link your rites to the various types discussed.

TABLE 3.1 Classification of rites

Type of ritual	Explanation
Rites of purification	Rituals of cleansing, chasing away evil, e.g. chasing away of winter spirits (carnival in southern Germany)
Rites of passage	Mark transition from one stage of life to another, e.g. graduation
Rites of reversal	Rituals of symbolic inversion and change of normal rule, e.g. carnivals
Rites of conspicuous display	Display of objects with a high symbolic value, e.g. processions
Rites of conspicuous consumption	Rituals with an importance on consumption, such as exchange of gifts, importance of food, e.g. Harvest Festivals
Ritual dramas	Rituals which celebrate myths, legends or history, e.g. re-enactments
Rites of exchange	Rituals of commerce, gift giving and charity, e.g. fundraising events
Rites of competition	Contests ranging from games to sport, e.g. Olympics
De-valorisation of rites	Ritual to end events such as closing ceremonies

As with many classifications, the various types of rituals should not be considered as mutually exclusive. Particularly when we consider the importance of religion within various rites, we can see a transformation of rituals. For example, Easter has developed from a purely religious festival to include rites of conspicuous consumption, reflected in the importance given to Easter eggs and chocolate. In addition, classifying rituals does not necessarily reflect and present their specific meanings. Galt (1973: 326) discusses how a carnival on the island of Pantelleria, Italy represents 'a mechanism by which solidarity is emphasised' in that locals celebrate a community solidarity which is not necessarily reflected in their daily life. It could be argued that this represents a form of 'change of normal rule', and thus a rite of reversal, however the real meaning is hidden until one partakes and gains insight into the ritual.

Religion and ritual

Another facet of the social world that is allied to ritual is religion, as it is often through specific symbolic behaviour that religion comes alive. Regardless of our personal religious beliefs we can look at most religions and see that they try to explain and deal with things that we find difficult in life. For example, we can ask why women have to endure pain during childbirth. We can find a biological answer to this question, but some of the world's religions also provide an explanation in the stories they tell. In the Christian religion, for example, pain in childbirth is a punishment handed down by God because of the bad behaviour by Eve in the Garden of Eden. This story is a myth.

Durkheim (1915) argues that myths are used to solve problems but do not succeed in doing so. Myths are not solely derived from religious contexts of course, but many religious celebrations and events are based on mythical elements. For an example of a religious ritual, which is celebrated regularly, we can again turn to Christianity. In many practices of Christianity the taking of Holy Communion is an integral part of affirming one's religious identity. Taking Holy Communion involves the taking of bread and wine as part of a ceremony conducted by a priest. The bread and wine are not consumed based on a need to satisfy hunger and thirst but to express belief, and the bread and wine stand for or symbolise something (in this case the blood and body of Christ); that is they are not simply bread and wine. The people taking part in the ceremony share the understanding of what the bread and wine mean and thus are publicly expressing that they share that understanding with the other people participating in the ritual.

THINK POINT

List as many religious celebrations as you can think of. Think about whether they have ritualistic elements and consider whether they build on myths.

Myths often provide the elements for the development of a ritual. Falassi (1987) discussed various types of rituals (as outlined in Table 3.1) and classifies the celebration of myths, for example through retelling of myths and legends as 'ritual dramas'.

Victor Turner (1969: 19) argued that the type of practices attached to religion meant that ritual could be described as 'prescribed formal behaviour for occasions not given over to technological routine, having references to beliefs in mystical beings or powers'. In this definition of ritual our understanding of what ritual is becomes linked to religion. However, as mentioned above, some people engage in rituals not because they have religious belief but because they are taking part in an expected form of behaviour. Similarly, not all rituals are connected to religion. In the modern world, although the role of religion has become less important (see chapter 2), there are nevertheless still many 'events' that have a basis in religious belief, for example:

THINK POINT

Every 25 December the majority of people in the UK exchange presents and then sit down together for a big lunch or dinner. This is often in small family units or with members of the extended family – aunts, uncles, cousins – and sometimes friends. The celebration is Christmas Day and, although we can look at the celebrations that took place at this time of year pre-Christianity, it is generally accepted that Christmas Day is a celebration of the birth of Christ. However, does everyone who takes part in the festivities believe in the Bible stories about Jesus or identify her/himself as Christian? Discuss and justify your answer.

At the same time there are events that can be understood as ritual but without a connection to religion, rather they are what is known as secular rituals. Before exploring what these are in more detail we want to examine some of the elements that are argued to make up ritual practices.

Rituals as rites of passage

Ritual practices have most famously been explored in the classic work of Arnold van Gennep (1909) *Les Rites de passage* (translated into English as *Rites of Passage*, 1960). Van Gennep's work examined a number of rites from around the world and from this he identified that, as well as rites that mark the passage of time (e.g. New Year), there are also rites that celebrate changes of social status. In drawing attention to the many rites that exist, and the importance attached to them, van Gennep highlighted the importance of transition and so made rites of passage a special category with three sub-categories: *rites of separation, transition rites* and *rites of incorporation* (Thomassen, 2012, see also Thomassen 2009).

Van Gennep's ideas were developed most notably by the British social anthropologist Victor Turner. In particular Turner explored the concept of liminality that van Gennep had developed in relation to both the 'middle' phases of all rites, and in particular in reference to rites of transition. Liminality can be considered as a situation or circumstance which is characterised by an uncertainty between past and traditional elements and future outcomes. The significance of Turner's work is that 'in his analysis of Ndembu ritual, Turner (1967, 1969, 1974) showed how ritual passages served as moments of creativity that freshened up the societal make-up, and ... that rituals were much more than mere reflections of social order' (Thomassen 2012: 23). In so doing Turner emphasised the importance of the liminal phase of rites and linked them to ideas of performance (see chapter 4) as well as exploring rites as times of potential. During the liminal phase of a ritual people are 'betwixt and between' statuses, or on the threshold of a new status, and therefore they have the possibility to change from their old status before the rite took place into something different after the rite.

Many events are based around celebrations of 'rites of passage' such as graduations, weddings and celebrations which acknowledge one's coming of age. As we have seen, van Gennep argued that rites of passage are practices that occur at times and places of transition. We can think about this idea of transition in relation to, for example, leaving childhood and becoming a teenager and then moving on to adulthood; from being a student to a graduate. As we change status or social category (child to adult) we want to mark this change with some sort of celebration or form of initiation. These celebrations or initiations are rites that van Gennep identified and classified into four types of social movement:

1 The passage of people from one *status* to another, e.g. marriage (moving from fiancé/e to wife or husband), initiation ceremonies bring someone from outside to inside a group.
2 The passage from one *place* to another, e.g. moving home.
3 The passage from one *situation* to another, e.g. starting a new job, school, going to university.
4 The passage of *time* – usually the whole social group moves from one period to another, e.g. New Year, new government or ruling authority (king/queen/emperor).

THINK POINT

List the transition periods in your life and how you or the people around you celebrate them.

Your answer might include some of the following: birth, marriage, christening, naming ceremonies, bar mitzvah, initiations, going on holiday, sporting fixtures, award ceremonies, New Year celebrations such as Hogmanay, Hanuka, Diwali, Eid al-Fitr, Halloween, high school proms. From this we can identify a number of different rites of passages:

• *Naming rites* – mark transition from non-person to person, from person outside a community to inside.
• *Initiation rites* – mark transition from one status to the next.
• *Marriage rites* – mark transition from single to married status, joining of families, partnership.
• *Funeral rites* – mark transition from person to ancestor, from present world to beyond.

THINK POINT

Explore different cultural practices in relation to the rites listed above. Find out information about the customs and ceremonies attached to each. What are the similarities and what are the differences?

CASE STUDY: *BUSAR* – INITIATION TRADITIONS IN ICELANDIC *GYMNASIA*

Gunnell (2007) examines rituals that take place in relation to the school year. He notes that due to the timing of the school calendar the ritual year is different in schools from other ritual timetables. For example the ritual year begins in September and ends in June/July for schools, rather than beginning with New Year in January and ending with Christmas in December. Gunnell explored rituals that have developed in Icelandic *gymnas* (secondary/high schools). He begins with initiation customs, which find parallels with Swedish and German *gulnäbb* (yellow nose), Estonian 'fox dubbing' and French *bizutage* (hazing).

In terms of the history of the rites, Gunnell notes that they have not undergone much change over time. Information from the eighteenth and nineteenth centuries suggests that some activities were 'imported' from Denmark:

> The earliest detailed account is from 1828 and describes the customs at the school in Bessastaðir (outside Reykjavik), and tells how new boys were assembled in a classroom late one night, and addressed by a caped figure in strange glasses, who called upon Óðinn and read them a grand speech about silence and other virtues. After this the so-called 'busar' were taken out and forcibly ducked in the local lake. Only then were they regarded as 'proper students'. (Gunnell 2007: 289)

Since this time, as one would expect, the education system in Iceland has developed and different types of schools opened, which led to variances in some of the traditions. Gunnell has identified some common features:

Preparation – this is in the earliest days of the new school year and can last for a week with the *busadagur* taking place on the Friday. During this time the *busar* (the new pupils) must follow particular pathways which have been marked out for them with tape and they can also be bought and sold by older pupils in order to undertake chores such as bag carrying and making notes. These elements have the effect of marking the new students as outsiders and different.

Busadagur – in many schools the older pupils work at night to make the communal student areas ready for the *busar* on the next day. Typical preparations include blacking out windows and creating obstacle courses for the *busar* to navigate upon their arrival the next day. Incense, music and candlelight might also be used. The initiators (the older students) dress up. Costumes adopted include executioners, American soldiers, vampires, punks, Greek elders or the wearing of a black bin liner. The *busar* or initiants are sometimes given instructions about what they need to wear, for example arriving in school with underpants on their heads, cross-dressed or in old clothes. On arrival at school they are further marked with face paint, a stamp or cardboard sign. The initiant can then enter the school via the obstacle course or by undertaking a series of challenges and must do their best to attend classes without being auctioned off to do work for older students.

Initiation – this usually occurs around midday and has two parts. The first is conducted in school and the second outside the school, usually in a natural setting. The school hall is often used for the inside section, and it is common for the whole school (not always including the teachers) to be present. The assembly of the whole school 'underlines the elements of dramatic "performance" and the social importance of the custom' (Gunnell 2007: 292; we will explore the issue of performance in the next chapter). During the time in the school hall the *busar* are further humiliated and ridiculed by the older students to emphasise their status as outsiders. The actual initiation takes place outside the school and involves a form of 'symbolic christening', using water that may have other 'ingredients' added to it, a mud bath or the kissing of a pig's head. Once this has been undertaken the *busar* can then enter the school as the equals of the other pupils.

Final acceptance – this might involve the sharing of a meal and/or a dance with the rest of the school.

The *Busadagur* ritual is not without its critics and controversies, especially with regard to the possible mistreatment of the younger students. Attempts to introduce more 'humane' practices are invariably met by students requesting a return to the 'traditional' methods. Pupils report the activities as among the most memorable of their teen years and the process is seen as not only initiating them into their new school but also serving to bond them as a year group. Gunnell (2007: 293) notes:

> the ritual year of the Icelandic *gymnas* begins with its own festival of ritual rebirth, a ceremony that contains many of the elements of initiation ceremonies known all over the world amongst native peoples: Ritual, death, cleansing, rebirth, and reeducation into secret lore.

He goes on to argue that the *Busadagur* events have a central social significance in Icelandic society. Such ceremonies do not exist at university level and can be seen to be more important than initiation ceremonies into, for example, the freemasons, which may occur later in life. The *Busadagur* 'are an initiation into a firm long-lasting social group as important as the personal family, which can go on to play a role in the formation of governments or the establishment of ties within the business world' (Gunnell 2007: 294).

(*Source*: Gunnell 2007)

Reflecting on the discussion on rites of passage and different forms of rituals, it becomes clear that many events celebrated today can be linked to rituals as cultural expressions. However, we have to acknowledge that rituals take place within a given context and have developed over time (see for example Barnett's 1949 article on the Easter festival). The development of rituals due to a changing political environment is discussed by Gilmore (1993), who explores the 'democratisation of ritual' by analysing how a carnival event in Andalusia has changed from how it was celebrated under Franco's dictatorship in 1973 to how it is celebrated in 1991, 15 years after democracy was introduced in Spain. Changes include new events, different timings, a change in expression and different forms of masquerade. Thus, ritual procedures and cultural expressions changed over time. This brings us to the next discussion point, namely the importance of certain scripts and specific artefacts in rituals.

Ritual scripts and artefacts

Often rituals follow specific procedures (e.g. a series of steps) and particular objects are needed for rituals to be carried out successfully, such as rings for a wedding. In his study of various rites of passage from around the world, van Gennep identified that certain characteristic patterns occurred in the order of the ceremonies:

- *Separation/pre-liminal* – the physical detachment of the participant from normal life. We can see this in the Icelandic example when the new pupils are only allowed to walk along marked pathways, which separates them from the spaces of movement used by the rest of the school's students and teachers.
- *Liminal/transitional* – the most important period according to Victor Turner, in which the participant is literally and symbolically marginalised. During this time the participants in the ritual have a sense of *communitas*. Communitas – a concept developed by Turner (1969) – is a feeling of camaraderie between those who are the focus of the ritual. So in the case study of the Icelandic schools the new pupils would feel a sense of bonding in their sharing of the same experiences – wearing odd clothes and participating in ordeals – before they become fully accepted into the life of the school.
- *Incorporation/post-liminal* – the participant is reincorporated into society/is returned to society. In the Icelandic case study this would be the final acceptance stage, which is celebrated with a meal or dance.

Victor Turner developed van Gennep's ideas to argue that all rites include these elements. So, in other words, each rite of passage has these elements within it, although some may be more developed than others depending on the purpose of the rite. So we would expect to see separation more clearly identified in a funeral.

Graduation ceremonies provide a good example of what we mean. The usual format of a graduation ceremony is a large gathering in a specially designated building or room. The students who have not yet graduated gather with their

FIGURE 3.2 Graduation celebrations
Source: © May Thazin.

guests – family and/or friends – at the venue. The majority of students will hire a gown and mortar board for the occasion. There is uniformity with regard to what is worn – black gowns, mortar boards and coloured hoods (see Figure 3.2). Changes occur with the level of degree so a PhD student will wear a different style and colour of gown. The students' guests are the audience for the ceremony and the students take their seats in a separate part of the venue. In this way the students are separated from their normal life and are on the threshold of becoming graduates. They no longer belong to the world of the student but neither are they part of the graduate community. All the students share the same status and likely the same sense of anticipation as they wait for their name to be called. It is during this liminal period that they will feel a sense of camaraderie with each other. After the ceremony is over the students – now graduates – return to their friends and family and rejoin their group with their new status.

In addition to a specific order, which many rituals follow, many rituals also rely on and feature specific objects needed to celebrate the ritual. If we consider some of the different ritual types identified in Table 3.1, such as 'rites of conspicuous display', 'rites of conspicuous consumption' and 'rites of exchange', it becomes clear that the rituals could not take place without an object. One thing common to many types of rites is food and drink. Rituals are often marked by the preparation and consumption of special food, such as wedding cakes or a special Christmas dinner, and the drinking of particular drinks, for example an expensive wine or champagne to signal celebration. This is further illustrated in the case study 'Drinking in Malta'.

CASE STUDY: DRINKING IN MALTA

Drinking alcohol is highly significant in Maltese culture, not only in the everyday but specifically during events such as saints' feasts and football celebrations. In the everyday, it is not unusual for wine to accompany a meal. Even children are often introduced to drinking wine on a daily basis from quite an early age. However, during public events, wine is notably absent and is replaced by chilled local beer or, for really special occasions, whisky.

Thus, even though drinking (of alcohol) takes place in the everyday, this is punctuated by a cycle of extraordinary drinking during special occasions (or events). Sundays are marked by an intensification of everyday drinking so that local adult men dominate many local bars. Particularly during the feast of St Paul these Sunday norms become even more intensified. During the days leading up to the main saint's day there are marches through the streets behind a brass band (the idea being to escort the band) involving drinking, visiting more than one bar and engaging in a round-buying system. The idea is to have a drink in each bar before moving on, but this inevitably breaks down, the round-buying system collapses and people carry their drinks with them. By the end the group escorting the band have become a drinking, dancing, singing crowd which might easily be found at a football match/rock concert rather than a religious festival.

(*Source*: Mitchell and Armstrong 2005)

However, in some instances, rites, and particularly initiation rites, are not linked to specific objects but rather to specific practices such as male/female circumcision, body piercing, tattooing and scarring. In other circumstances ritual is concerned with a particular place. This often forms the basis of pilgrimage or sacred journeys. There are many examples of these from around the world, including the Muslim pilgrimage to Mecca, the Hindu pilgrimage of the Four Dhams in India, Christian pilgrimages to Canterbury and Glastonbury in the UK, Our Lady of Guadalupe in Mexico, St Joseph's Oratory, Montreal and Santiago de Compostela, Spain and many more (Westwood 1997). The journey to the place may take several days, even weeks. It may be undertaken for a variety of reasons – to pay homage, to take healing waters or to take part in activities or events that celebrate the particular figure associated with the place. The case study and picture of St Winifred's Well (also spelt St Winefride's Well) illustrates the point.

Up until now many of the rites that we have identified relate to religious rituals, which demonstrates the close relationship between various rituals and religious beliefs. These types of activities relate to the sacred. They are used as a method of organising the social world, of identifying groups and individuals and their roles in society. However, not all events that structure and organise the social world are

CASE STUDY: ST WINIFRED'S WELL

St Winifred's shrine is in the town of Holywell (Treffynnon in Welsh), Flintshire, North Wales. It is a Catholic shrine to St Winifred, marking the spot where she died (in the seventh century) and, according to the story, caused a spring to rise. The spring waters emerge to form a large pool of water believed to have healing properties. The shrine is open all year and visitors come to the site to bathe and collect the water. However, it is also associated with particular events, including daily religious services between Pentecost (the fiftieth day after Easter) and 30 September, and two further events. The first is the Annual National Pilgrimage in June, which involves a procession through the town of Holywell, and an annual Pan-Orthodox pilgrimage on the first Saturday in October.

(*Source*: Hulse 1997)

based in religion, for example, the initiation ceremony and graduation example discussed above. 'Rites of competition' and 'de-valorisation of rites' are considered secular rites and will now be discussed in more detail.

FIGURE 3.3 Pilgrims queuing to kiss the relic at St Winifred's Well, North Wales

Source: © Hazel Andrews.

Secular rituals

As social life has developed through the phase of modernisation (see chapter 2) we have seen a decline in the importance of the sacred. Sally Moore and Barbara Myerhoff (1977: 3) noted that the study of ritual had been mainly in the context of religion and magic: 'the association between those formalities we call "ritual" and their religious or magical purposes has been so strong that analysis of the two has almost invariably proceeded together'. They go on to argue that there are some ceremonies that do not have a basis in the sacred but are situated in the non-sacred or secular/profane world but are nevertheless very powerful. If we view the sacred and secular worlds as different entities then 'it is possible to analyze the ways in which ceremony and ritual are used in the secular affairs of modern life' (Moore and Myerhoff 1977: 3).

There are many events in the social world that may not appear at first sight to fit neatly into the category of ritual because they do not have a religious association that can be understood in this way. As Moore and Myerhoff (1977: 4) assert: 'secular ceremonies are common in industrial societies and are found in all contexts. . . . Meetings, court trials . . . and other formal assemblies of many kinds are part of the ordinary fabric of collective social life.' Stevenson and Alaug (2000: 459) argue that: 'beyond being contests, sports are events with repetitive, stylized, elaborate structures that transmit symbolic messages'. While there is therefore no obvious sacred element to sport, the presence of symbols 'convey[s] important symbolic messages about the nature of society' (Stevenson and Alaug 2000: 457). This is because, Stevenson and Alaug (2000: 468) contend: 'sports events are effective symbol conveyors because they create the ritual environment that makes people receptive to these messages'. That is, sporting events often encourage heightened emotional states as people get behind their team or an individual competitor.

There are many examples making the comparison between modern sporting events and ritual (e.g. Patterson 1969; Arens 1976; Leach 1976; Cheska 1978; Foley 1990 – all cited in Stevenson and Alaug, 2000). Stevenson and Alaug (2000: 459) point to the work of Salter (1977) concerning Eastern Woodlands Indians, demonstrating that:

> Iroquois lacrosse matches were ritual events . . . [and that] although the game was at the heart of the event and winning the contest was meaningful to the competitors, the match results were insignificant when compared to the event's broader social messages.

Stevenson and Alaug (2000: 460) go on to argue that 'viewed as events, sports' secular ritual qualities, especially message transmission, become apparent'. They develop their ideas in relation to football in Yemen (see case study 'Football in newly united Yemen').

CASE STUDY: FOOTBALL IN NEWLY UNITED YEMEN – RITUAL OF EQUITY, IDENTITY AND STATE FORMATION

At one time Yemen was split into two separate countries but it underwent unification in 1990. Before this, both independent states had a history of football playing. Sports were not actively encouraged until both states became republics in the 1970s and the respective governments recognised the symbolic value of local and national teams. 'As the most popular and widely played sport, football has been particularly emblematic of popular sentiments, and the symbols attached to football clubs parallel the political histories of the two republics and the united state' (Stevenson and Alaug 2000: 462).

In the now-united Yemen, football matches are held on a regular basis in stadia run by local authorities. The largest stadium holds about 10,000 spectators on open seating. The ticket price is comparatively cheap and is set nationally by a government ministry. Stevenson and Alaug note (2000: 460) 'as in many countries . . . football in Yemen is an expression of male dominance or hegemony'. The games are popular and often reach stadium capacity, with fans flag-waving, shouting, cheering and criticising their team. 'The most dedicated fans decorate their cars or businesses with team colors' (Stevenson and Alaug 2000: 461). The passion felt by some fans at important matches may mean that fights break out.

Following unification a national football team was established, with players drawn equally from the former two republics. The priority was to ensure that both former republics were represented equally and that the players would play as a unified team. The government was not concerned with winning the Eleventh Asian Games (1990), in which the team participated, but rather in symbolically demonstrating the unification of the two republics in the players picked for the national team. However, because the games were not broadcast in Yemen they drew little attention.

A second national tournament team was formed, again with a fairly equal selection of players from both former republics. It played its first game in 1991. This team garnered more interest and was broadcast both on radio and television. The event was opened with the playing of the national anthem and the parade of the team onto the field. 'When the Yemeni side scored, the crowd erupted in cheers for the team and unification' (Stevenson and Alaug 2000: 466). The country's president made a personal phonecall to congratulate the team on its winning performance. The game and the elements of ritual that accompanied it showed that the government of the new country was committed to unification. It was more successful than the Asian Games because it was visible, thus allowing the citizens to view for themselves elements of the united republics – the flying of the country's new flag at the football stadium, the opening of the game with the new national anthem and the wearing of new national football kit by the players. All these served to symbolise and to help construct a new sense of Yemeni identity.

(*Source*: Stevenson and Alaug 2000)

As we know there are certain events like the Olympic Games and football World Cup that occur on a regular basis, which follow certain scripts and involve specific objects. The Olympic Games always has opening and closing ceremonies, with the Olympic torch presenting the key artefact of the Games along with, for example, medals. This gives a sense of tradition, the idea that something is done because that is the way it has always been done and we should not deviate from that. This leads to the next point, concerning the way in which some events give the impression of longevity but are quite recent.

Invented tradition and events

There are many aspects of rituals, ceremonies and celebrations that we think of as always having been the way they are today, and there are many festivals that give the impression that they are deeply rooted in times past. However, this is not always the case and this leads us to consider the ideas put forward by Eric Hobsbawm and Terence Ranger (1983) in their book *The Invention of Tradition*. Traditions relate to practices and things that have been inherited; that is, it is often believed that their origins are deeply rooted in the past and that their practice has always been undertaken in a certain way. They are social constructs that are often used to reinforce or maintain power relations, social ideals and values in the present by reference to a past which may or may not be historically accurate. Hobsbawm and Ranger (1983:1) attest that: '"Traditions" which appear or claim to be old are often quite recent in origin and sometimes invented.' They argue that such traditions have a specific form and purpose.

> 'Invented tradition' is taken to mean a set of practices, normally governed by overtly or tacitly accepted rules and of a ritual or symbolic nature, which seek to inculcate certain values and norms of behaviour by repetition, which automatically implies continuity with the past … where possible, they normally attempt to establish continuity with a suitable historic past.
>
> (Hobsbawm and Ranger 1983: 1)

These points link us back to the discussion about the role of events in society as ways by which social status can be reinforced by the practice of some events.

THINK POINT

You have been asked to plan a traditional white wedding. What elements must you include to ensure that it lives up to the idea of being traditional? Where do these ideas originate?

The connection between the invention of traditions and events is that some events are invented. As Boissevain (2008: 32) notes 'festivals . . . are being invented, borrowed, reinvented and modified and linked to tradition or history by government, commercial or civic groups promoting their own agendas'. He cites the example noted by Fournier (2007) of celebrations for the picking of green olives in a Provençal village. The village mayor arranged a bullfight and a dance in order to promote the village and its produce. Thirty years following its establishment the event has grown to include a number of activities including, among others, an antique car show, concerts and local craft displays, and 'the local olives now scarcely figure in the celebration' (Fournier 2008: 34). We can understand further the idea of inventing activities by examining another case study within a sporting ritual, that of the torch relay for the Olympic Games.

CASE STUDY: THE TORCH RELAY – REINVENTION OF TRADITION AND CONFLICT WITH THE GREEKS

Writing in relation to the winter Olympics, hosted in Lillehammer, Norway, in 1994, Klausen argues that the torch relay was exploited by various Norwegian-based interest groups. First we might note that Klausen argues that the Olympic Games are secular rituals following a codified set of rules that can be compared to religious service books. Practices around the Olympic flame are governed by Rule 60 of the Olympic charter. In 1994 plans were set for a torch relay that brought about tensions between Norway and Greece.

In an earlier winter Olympics (1952), the Norwegians had brought a flame from Morgedal (known as the 'cradle of skiing') to Oslo. This was not recognised by the International Olympic Committee (IOC) as the official flame as is it did not originate in Olympia, Greece. The Norwegians were keen to see the flame in Morgedal adopted as the official winter Olympic flame. Although this was never accepted by the IOC, in 1994 attempts were again made to endow the Norwegian flame with the same status as the one originating in Greece. The plan was to bring the flame from Morgedal to Oslo where it was to be mixed with the flame from Greece and then taken to the stadium in Lillehammer. This change in proceedings, Klausen (1999b: 77) says: 'was a re-invention of the semi-tradition invented in Oslo back in 1952'. The idea behind this was, according to Klausen, to highlight Norway as a modern nation with solid traditional roots. Underpinning the ideas of longevity was 'how much importance the Norwegians attach to the right of ownership of the skiing tradition' (Klausen 1999b: 85). However, this came into conflict with Greek ideas of ownership in relation to the Olympic flame. The flame that originates in Greece is seen as the pure, authentic flame, and the Hellenic Olympic Committee claims rights over it; there was talk of a Greek boycott of the games.

The solution to the conflict was found in the granting of permission for the Morgedal flame to complete the journey to the centre of Lillehammer and be received the day before the opening ceremony. The Greek flame arrived in a village near to Lillehammer and was taken to the opening ceremony. The flame from Morgedal remained burning in Lillehammer and was used to light the main torch in the stadium for the opening of the Paralympics. Although the attempt to reinvent the tradition of the lighting of the Olympic flame had not succeeded, the Norwegians did not give up. Following the games they made representation to the IOC to request that the Norwegian *budstikke* (an ancient Norwegian method of communication, the oldest form being a piece of wood with a carved message; in the case of the Olympic Games it was carried by a representative of the Norwegian post office acting as escort to the Morgedal flame bearer) become an official feature of the torch relay for the Winter Olympic Games.

(*Source*: Klausen 1999b)

Summary

In this chapter we explored:

- understandings of rituals as function and process;
- the different types of rites of passage and their components;
- the difference between secular and religious rituals;
- how rituals can be used to give a sense of longevity and rootedness.

Suggested reading

Hobsbawm, E. and Ranger, T. (1983) *The Invention of Tradition*. Cambridge: Cambridge University Press.
Moore, S. and Myerhoff, B. (eds) (1977) *Secular Ritual*. Amsterdam: Van Gorcum.
Van Gennep, A. (1960) *The Rites of Passage*. Chicago: University of Chicago Press.
Turner, V. (1969) *The Ritual Process*. Harmondsworth: Penguin.
Westwood, J. (1997) *Sacred Journeys: Paths for the New Pilgrim*. London: Gaia Books.

Useful websites

Pagan Pride: http://www.paganpride.org.uk

Calendar of Cultural and Religious Dates: http://www.immi.gov.au/living-in-australia/a-multicultural-australia/calendar-australia

St Winifred's Well: http://www.saintwinefrideswell.com

4

EVENTS PERFORMANCES

This chapter will:

- consider events as performances;
- explore the role of the event consumer as performer;
- critically discuss the role of performance theory and construction of narratives in the event experience;
- discuss notions of social capital, and authenticity.

Among other things, events are constructed through design and event objectives and, on the other hand, through socio-cultural dynamics such as power relationships between stakeholders. We can refer to this interplay of various elements as the social construction of events. Acknowledging these underlying dynamics does not detract from the fact that essentially events are acts of different performances. Particularly if we acknowledge performance as an 'inclusive term', as suggested by Schechner (1988) and illustrated in Figure 4.1, we are able to see how the contemporary understanding of and approach to events can be enhanced by bridging discussion between events and performance.

As seen in Figure 4.1, various forms and approaches that we have so far discussed such as rites, ceremonies, ritualisation and practices in everyday life, sports and entertainments, are clearly linked to performance. Yet, if we begin to discuss performance and events more deeply, we could begin to ask a range of questions. For example: Who are the performers at events? What roles do the audience play in an event performance and are spectators part of the event performance? What role does consumption play in an event performance? How do contested event performances fit into the picture? What role does the body play in event performances? And what role do narratives play within the construction of event performances? To attempt to find answers to these questions,

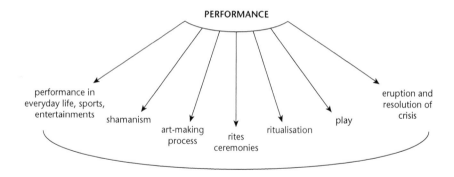

FIGURE 4.1 Performance fan (adapted from Schechner 1988)

it is necessary to first gain an understanding of the key terminology that we are using in this chapter.

Performance:

Performance can be considered as a representative and/or symbolic activity, such as a ritual or theatrical performance. Essentially a performance is an act/action, which presents some form of activity, which might be in the form of entertainment, generally for the benefit of someone else.

Performance study:

The study of performance has developed from a focus on mainly symbolic approaches, such as understanding dramas, to analysing the process of these practices and performances, while acknowledging that the study of performance is largely about the creation of present realities.

Performer:

A human or non-human (animal) being that presents and/or takes part in a performance. Generally the term 'performer' refers to active participants in a performance.

Performativity:

Performativity is used to describe verbal and non-verbal forms of expression. Thus, it does not refer to a specific event but rather refers to how someone expresses, behaves and reacts in different situations in daily life.

The event as a performance

Turner (1987: 11) argues that performances are never open-ended but rather have a 'beginning, a sequence of overlapping but isolable phases and an end. But their structure is not that of an abstract system; it is generated out of the dialectical oppositions of processes and of levels of process.' Clearly, this statement can also be applied to events in that they are scheduled happenings which have a beginning, a sequence of phases and an end. Regardless of the length of time that might pass between the beginning and the end (for example, ranging from a five-minute street performance to the Olympics, which can last up to 21 days, or other events which are even longer), there is always a start and an end point of an event. With reference to the Easter holiday celebrations, Barnett (1949) notes that the festival period can last from several days to several weeks, depending on the contextual setting. Clearly, not all opening and closing acts are celebrated, and so many go unnoticed. Some of the best-known opening and closing celebrations are of course the Olympics (e.g. Puijk 1999), which have gained increased significance over the years, with cultural, national, local, political and other messages being important elements in different performances which constitute the ceremony. We have touched on the social significance of the Olympics in chapter 2 and in chapter 3 considered ideas relating to the invention of traditions in connection to the opening ceremony of the winter Olympics in 1994. We would like to illustrate the importance of the opening and closing acts in more detail in the case study concerning the Beijing Olympics.

CASE STUDY: 'BEIJING OLYMPICS OPENS WITH SPECTACULAR CEREMONY'

This newspaper headline is only one of many which discuss the importance and significance of the Olympic Opening and Closing Ceremonies. The Opening Ceremony in Beijing presented a performance of 'China's millennia of history and hi-tech present'. Over 10,000 performers took part, approximately 91,000 people saw it live at the Stadium and an estimated 1 billion people watched it on television. While the 2008 Olympics are considered one of the most politicised Games since the Cold War, with protests throughout the run-up and the actual Games, the Opening Ceremony is considered to have played a significant role in diverting many people's attention away from political issues.

> At once a glittering, showy extravaganza and a patriotic demonstration of pride in 5,000 years of recorded history, the opening ceremony was timed to start at eight minutes past 8pm on August 8, reflecting the number's status in China as a bearer of good fortune. It took in everything from giant written scrolls and a representation of the Great Wall formed by thousands of performers to spacemen floating from the stadium roof, symbolising one of China's most recent technological achievements.
> (Walker 2008)

As always, the ceremony ended with the lighting of the Olympic flame, following an Olympic Flame Relay which saw many political protests around the world.

(*Source*: Walker 2008)

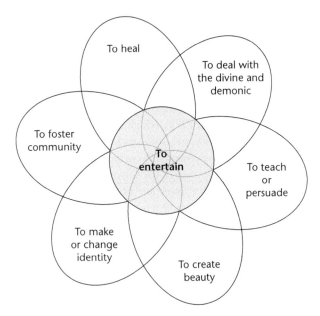

FIGURE 4.2 The seven interlocking spheres of performance (adapted from: Schechner 2003)

In our opening chapter we explored different event types and forms. We are able to expand this initial exploration by acknowledging Schechner's (2003) discussion of the different functions of performance, which are illustrated in Figure 4.2.

Clearly, most events can be differentiated by what they are trying to achieve. As seen in Figure 4.2, performances can take on different functions, all of which can be applied to the event context. It is important, of course, to recognise that the spheres are not separate from each other but rather present a coherent and inter-linked form, which allows for a performance and event to have different functions at the same time.

THINK POINT

The Royal Wedding of Prince William was celebrated with small street parties in many communities throughout Britain. Consider the functions of and reasons for these events. Which of Schechner's (2003) interlocking spheres can be applied to this context?

The functions identified by Schechner (2003) can of course be expanded and rephrased to change the approach to other performances, such as cultural and social performances or secular folk holidays, which could for example also be embedded in Schechner's functions of entertainment, dealing with the divine and the demonic and fostering of a community. The contemporary event context has furthered the discussion of the various functions of events, centring much of the attention on a more economic approach while acknowledging the need to provide unique experiences. Indeed, many events are organised for financial reasons, which can range from making a profit to raising money for charities. This latter function as a fundraising event can come about for a number of different reasons, as explained by Webber (2004: 123). These are the development of donors; extra income from the current donor base; thanking current supporter base; an excuse to write to a group of current supporters; social or community-based occasions; acquisition of new support; looking after current donors; networking for attendees; and maintaining brand name, especially for large household-name charities. Coming back to Figure 4.2, many events have different functions, of which some are more or less important; for example, fostering a community can be the main reason to organise and hold an event, while at the same time organisers are trying to ensure good entertainment for everyone and the development of a communal identity as a result of the event. To link this discussion about the functions of events to the wider context of performance, we argue that events are stages in which different performances consisting of social interaction, processes and behaviours are taking place, directed by the underlying functions of the event context. These influence visitors' performances and ultimately the event experiences. Figure 4.3 shows the interaction

FIGURE 4.3 Interaction between performer and audience at the St Patrick's Day Parade, Dublin, 2010

Source: © Teresa Leopold.

that took place between performers and audience of the St Patrick's Day Parade in Dublin in 2010.

Social interaction at events can create meaning through shared practice and understanding, so that all forms of performances contribute to the event experience (Deighton 1992).

CASE STUDY: FESTIVALS OF MOORS AND CHRISTIANS, BENEIXAMA SPAIN

Krom (2008) uses some of Schechner's (2003) ideas about performance to examine festivals of Moors and Christians in southern Spain, in particular at Beneixama, Alicante. There are many festivities which combine both religious and secular elements. They are community celebrations with a focus on expressions of local identity, but have also been part of processes of commodification. Krom (2008: 119) argues 'that the performative character of the celebration constitutes the foundation for both its marketability and its efficacy as an emblem of local identity'.

The history of the festivals relates to the reclaiming of the Iberian Peninsula from the Moors by the Christians. They involve religious ceremonies and the re-enactment of fictional or non-fictional historical scenes. All sorts of activities take place, including: parades, processions, dancing, battles, fireworks, rifle shooting. The celebrations last for three to five days and include many local people. The events held in Beneixama are considered to be among the oldest of their kind and last for several days. The festivities involve flag raising, hymn singing, musical presentations, the celebration of mass, parades of the Christian and Moorish companies, offerings to saints and street battles.

In terms of performance Krom argues that the festival is a 'perfect example of performance, of what Schechner calls 'showing doing'; what is meant by 'showing doing' is to display 'doing' (Schechner 2006, in Krom 2008: 122). Schechner (2006, in Krom 2008: 122) identifies performance in everyday life and Krom argues that the festivals of the Moors and Christians provide a good example of this type of performance because participation begins at an early age and 'is one way by which appropriate social and cultural behaviour is learned and transmitted'.

Drawing on Schechner's (2003) contention that all performances have some basic features in common, Krom examines the festival of Moors and Christians in more depth, beginning with Time.

Time – Performances can be seen to organise time and three types of time are identified: *clock*, *event* and *symbolic*. In the events at Beneixama real *clock* time refers to how many days, for example, the celebrations have lasted (sometimes up to ten). There is a predetermined timetable for the festival programme but this takes place in *event* time, which refers to an activity that must take place at a particular point in the programme regardless of the *clock* time. For the festival this *event* time can be applied to the opening parade and all the parades and processions on the other days. Regardless of the *clock* time these activities must go ahead. *Symbolic* time makes reference to another time span. For example, the negotiations between the Moors and Christians enacted through the recital of poetry make reference to the actual time that the negotiations would have been conducted. Similarly, the religious masses held as part of the celebrations refer to different understandings of time – eternity and life after death.

Props – Although Schechner (2003) argues that the props or objects used for events generally have little monetary and material value outside of the event, Krom contradicts this by noting that those used in the Festival of the Moors and Christians are expensive: for example, the jewels used on one of the religious icons and some of the costumes. Regardless of the monetary value, the props are important symbolically and often play a central role in the celebrations. For example, a giant effigy used in similar festivals in Biar and Villena has much more symbolic value than monetary worth.

Rules and places – The whole village is given over to the celebrations and Krom (2008: 126) notes 'it [is] impossible to escape the festival'. However, there are special places which are the focus of particular activities, for example the church and the square in front of the church. At the same time there are separate spaces for some more private aspects of the event, for example the night before the festival begins the members of the groups forming the different parade assemblages meet privately in their respective headquarters for a joint meal.

(*Source*: Krom 2008)

Social vs. cultural performances

Performance can also be classed into 'social' and 'cultural' categories (Turner 1987). To explain further, similar to our argument in chapter 1 that the term 'event' can also refer to daily life occurrences such as deaths and births, performances are not just planned and enacted happenings such as theatre plays and music concerts – our daily social life can also be described as a succession of different performances. Think, for example, about your lecture setting as a stage set where the lecturer and the students take on different roles depending on teaching style. A traditional lecture style would thus mean that the lecturer would be the key performer with students acting as the audience. In workshop or tutorial sessions, students often take a much larger role 'on stage' (in the classroom) by participating in discussions and debates. In assessment scenarios, students would often become the main performers through, for example, assessed presentations, while the lecturer becomes the audience. Another example is your different behaviour depending on the social situation in which you find yourself. Deighton (1992) suggests that in sales situations the person wanting to purchase a product and the sales person take on specific roles in the sales performance, such as asking and answering questions. Within such an exchange, there is often a strong awareness that the sales person performs and communicates in a certain, often calculated, way.

THINK POINT

Reflect on your own experiences – do you behave (perform) differently when spending time with your parents than when you spend time with your friends? Why are you performing in different situations in certain ways? What role does the 'stage set', that is, your immediate environment, play in your performance? What different roles do you perform in your daily life?

Turner (1987: 13) explains these social life performances by arguing that our 'Self is presented through the performance of roles, through performance that breaks roles, and through declaring to a given public that one has undergone a transformation of state and status, been saved or damned, elevated or released.' In other words, social performance is largely linked to how we present ourselves in everyday life. Goffman (1959) pioneered much of the early discussion regarding this perspective and argued for a holistic approach for understanding acting or performances where all perspectives of and influences on a situation need to be considered. To apply this to the event context, we need to explore the role of the performer, the setting of an event, which Goffman refers to as the front and back stage, and the role of the audience as watching a performance but also as taking part in a performance. Deighton (1992) similarly highlighted four event-related links between the consumer (or the audience) and performance: first, consumers attend performances; second, consumers participate in performances; third, consumers perform with products; and, fourth, products perform for consumers. Exploring all these facets will thus help us to illustrate the links between performance studies and the contemporary event context more clearly.

THINK POINT

When does the audience become part of the performance? Consider improvisational theatre, also known as improv, which refers to performances where actors are not working with a script but rather direct their performance through suggestions provided by the audience. Think about the different performers during an improvisation theatre performance. How is the audience partaking in the performance? What is the role of the audience?

Cultural performance and social performance are not necessarily mutually exclusive if we consider specific cultural performances which take place in our daily social life. For example, consider the cultural performance of forming orderly queues when waiting for a bus, which is common in the UK but not in other nations. Clearly, this could be considered as both a cultural but also a social performance. However, often a cultural performance also refers to stage performances, cultural festivals and other cultural events. Thus, in this chapter we will explore from different angles how performance studies can be used to shed light on the cultural and social processes that take place during an event.

Contextualising performances

In order to understand and develop the meaning of a performance or an event, we have to contextualise them within their wider setting. To further explain what we mean by the contextualisation or decontextualisation of performance: contextualisation refers to the idea that performances can only be really understood if the context in which they are taking place is also taken into consideration, so that the situational context of events becomes important (Bauman and Brigg 1990). Decontextualisation thus refers to the processes of understanding the various elements in isolation from the context, which constitutes a setting and, in our case, an event. Bauman and Briggs (1990: 69) suggest: 'Contextualisation involves an active process of negotiation in which participants reflexively examine the discourse as it is emerging, embedding assessments of its structure and significance in the speech itself.' Good examples that illustrate the need for constant contextualisation during events are comedy clubs or political rallies. In those contexts, performers 'on stage' continuously assess the influence their performance might have upon the audience before deciding on the next step in their performance. Acknowledging that every attendee and/or performer sees and understands situations differently, depending on their background, identity, knowledge, etc., each performance can be contextualised slightly differently. The case study on the growth of Halloween in Norway illustrates the complexity of events when considering their context. The cultural setting, as discussed above, but also cultural norms and behaviour, form part of the contextualisation of an event setting.

As the case study states, Paul Walker is an American and therefore used to annual celebrations of Halloween. In the United States the occasion has been marked by festivities for a number of years which have been developed in different ways. For example Figures 4.4. and 4.5 demonstrate how the people of Park City, Utah,

CASE STUDY: GROWTH OF HALLOWEEN IN NORWAY

An American man named Paul Walker (a pseudonym) employed in Norway during the 1990s decided to celebrate Halloween one year in the way in which he was used to doing in the United States in the form of a Halloween party. He invited his Norwegian friends. Before the party took place he received a number of enquiries from his friends regarding dress code, the history of Halloween and general information as to what the party was for. He received so many enquiries that he needed to make a message for his telephone answering machine which gave the information that the invitees were looking for: a history of Halloween, how it could be celebrated and the dress code. From this experience he decided to start a business venture.

Halloween was not celebrated in Norway in the same way in which it was in the United States so, effectively, Walker had identified a market opening. 'If the celebration of this holiday was to succeed, however, people needed to know how the holiday could be celebrated, why they should celebrate it, and also when the celebration should take place' (Ohrvik 2007: 103). The result was the establishment of a website which gave the historical background to Halloween and had links to information about where to buy costumes, find more information, lists of Halloween events around the country, recipes for the occasion, as well as photos of Norwegian Halloween celebrations. The interest in and success of the website led Walker to become an 'event maker' (Ohrvik 2007: 105) through the establishment of his own company, which developed links with bars and restaurants as venues for parties. A central element of the parties was dressing up and receiving prizes for the best costume. Walker identified a number of props necessary for the successful performance of the event script. These included the importance of dressing up and changing identity. 'Halloween was an occasion that gave people an opportunity to be someone or something else, and to play a different role in the social system' (Ohrvik 2007: 105). The parties included entertainment for guests in the form of professional singers and actors, and the decoration of rooms. Walker's business grew because he was increasingly hired to organise 'proper' Halloween events.

However, not everyone in Norway was happy with the growth in the celebrations and protests emanated from different quarters of society, including government, based on the non-Christian and commercial elements of the festivities. Walker defended his position by claiming that his main concern was to raise awareness of a celebration that he felt the Norwegians needed in order to 'relax and be someone else'. The performances that Halloween allows the Norwegians to enact are aided by the use of 'props' – costumes, food, decorations – and Walker supplied a script. The script derived from the information he supplied on the website and was added to as he staged more of the events and used those experiences to develop the narrative around the festivities. Not all of the growth in Halloween activities can be attributed to Paul Walker; such entrepreneurs 'represent a kind of expertise that places them in a position in which they can organize, play, and manipulate the process of ritualization' (Ohrvik 2007: 107). However, this is not possible without the willingness of participants.

(*Source*: Ohrvik 2007)

adapted Halloween activities to reflect an apparent commonly held love of dogs within the community.

Cultural norms

Let us start with the question of how individuals learn the cultural roles that they should be playing or a particular cultural pattern that they should follow as part of an event. Different cultures perform differently. Turner (1987: 13) explains this by suggesting:

FIGURE 4.4 Howl-O-Ween Pet Parade, Park City, Utah, 2008 #1

Source: © Martha Noyes.

FIGURE 4.5 Howl-O-Ween Pet Parade, Park City, Utah, 2008, #2

Source: © Martha Noyes.

There are various types of social performance and genres of cultural performance, and each has its own style, goals, entelechy [self-realisation, forces vital for reaching completion], rhetoric, developmental pattern and characteristic roles. These types and genres differ in different cultures, and in terms of the scale and complexity of the sociocultural fields in which they are generated and sustained.

THINK POINT

You are invited to your friend's wedding in another country, which you have little knowledge of. What do you need to find out before attending the wedding ceremony?

Often appropriate behaviour of individuals or groups at events is assumed to be a given, whether this is during a lively street event such as a parade, where participant might partake in dances, cheering and street performances, or a more spiritual event like a baptism where, depending on the religion and culture, the setting might require a quieter and more passive performance. Many of these behavioural norms are acquired through observations, during the event by copying other people's behaviour or through media, or learned over time. Of course we have to recognise that while people might partake in a certain event, the motivation for doing so might differ. For example, Barnett (1949: 63), who explores the development of the Easter holiday celebrations, argues that:

> However, it should be noted that though individuals learn the customary 'holiday culture' of their society, their personal motivations in 'acting out' given holiday roles may vary enormously. Thus a member of our society may attend church on Good Friday or Easter because he is a devout Christian, or believes he will be criticized if he fails to do so, or to exhibit new clothes. Individuals use standardized culture forms to implement and satisfy varied needs.

Another example is that people might attend wedding ceremonies to partake in an important celebration of a friend or family member, however do not believe in the institution of matrimony. This reiterates some of the discussion around ritual in chapter 3.

THINK POINT

Have you attended events for reasons that might be different from those of other attendees? How would you explain your performance during the event? Did you feel part of the event?

Communicating performances

The link between communication and performance is further illustrated when considering that communication 'refers to the practices, processes and mediums by which meanings are provided and understood in a cultural context' (Pritchard and Jaworski 2005: 2). Potential questions which emerge when considering the act of communication as part of a performance are: What is (are) the message(s) that is (are) being sent as part of a performance? How does the audience understand and interpret the message? How does the audience react to the message? How far do cultural differences influence the communication process? How is the message being communicated? And what channels and media are used to communicate during the event? Reflecting on these questions, it becomes clear that the communication during a performance can impact and influence the event and event experience.

We can argue that performances and events provide the frame (or stage) in which communication between the performer and the audience can take place. The success of the performance and event experiences is thus partly linked to the communicative process that takes place during the event, whether this is in the form of speeches, singing or acting, but also before the event, that is, through advertising. In addition, the setting and context in which an event or performance takes place can also influence its framing and goes beyond the pure communicative process which takes place (Bauman and Briggs 1990).

Different roles of audience and performer

We have established that a performance is an action for the benefit of someone else. Thus, it could be argued that for a performance to take place, there is the need for at least one performer and one audience member. Many events, however, consist of a range of different performers. This can be seen in Figure 4.6, a photo of the Chester Races, which shows different performances taking place at an event, including the audience watching and betting, the betting agents (or bookies) working and the jockeys racing.

Deighton (1992) moves beyond two existing taxonomies, which explore the differences between spectacle and contest (Barthes 1972, cited in Deighton 1992),

FIGURE 4.6 Different performances at the Chester races

Source: © Les Roberts.

and the distinction between spectacles, festivals and ceremonies (Dayan and Katz, cited in Deighton 1992). Rather than exploring the differences according to the type of performance, Deighton's new taxonomy increases the focus on the role that different performers might take. Thus, his central focus is on providing a tool to understand when a skill performance, thrill performance, show performance or festive performance, with reference to the consumer's role, takes place (see Figure 4.7). Central to this taxonomy is the recognition that the individual directs his or her involvement in the performance.

THINK POINT

Referring to Deighton's 'Strategies for emphasising dramatism' shown in Figure 4.7, have a look at the different event examples provided and think of events which you have attended with regard to skill performance, thrill performance, show performance and festive performance. How did the events' purposes and your role during the events influence your performances and experiences of these events?

As illustrated in Figure 4.7, whether an event audience is passive or active, whether the attention is on the actors or different focal points, and whether the audience takes on only a small active role or different roles in the performance influences

			Influences on the Consumer's Role	
			Emphasise Observer's Role • Passive and segregated audience • Focus on actors • Constrained set of audience responses	**Emphasise Participant's Role** • Involved, integrated audience • No single focus • Flexible audience roles
Influences on the Event's Purpose	**Emphasise Event's Realism**	• Naturalistic setting • Tension and uncertainty • Values under test	**SHOW PERFORMANCE** e.g. sport performances and competitions	**THRILL PERFORMANCE** e.g. class reunions, conventions
	Emphasise Event's Fantasy	• Artificial setting • Ritualistic • Predictable • Affirmation of values	**SHOW PERFORMANCE** e.g. theatre and opera performances	**FESTIVE PERFORMANCE** e.g. Halloween, Christmas

FIGURE 4.7 Strategies for emphasising dramatism (adapted from Deighton 1992)

their event experience. Thus, individuals' motivations and deviant behaviour at festivals are regarded as relevant to the study of understanding event consumers as performers, as both aspects influence an individual's own event experiences and have the potential to influence others' experiences. We will be discussing the role of experience in more detail below; what needs to be acknowledged within this discussion, however, is that regulation, structures, systems and norms that influence our daily life of course also influence our performance, such as certain expected behaviour at an event. Moore (1971, in Turner 1987: 10) suggests that while our social reality and social performance is largely fluid, social reality can temporarily become inflexible through structures and regulations. Security staff, stewards and other orderlies at events play an important role in ensuring a certain behavioural standard is maintained and regulations are obeyed (Figure 4.8). While these individuals 'only do their job' they thus can also have an influence on people's experiences of events.

Within this context we would like to draw your attention to Cynthia Enloe's (2000) ideas about the militarisation of everyday life. She describes how our lives are becoming more militarised through a 'subtle process', which is evident in everyday practices and goods, for example *Star Wars*-shaped pasta pieces in children's food or camouflage-look condoms. Enloe (2000: 289) argues that 'militarization

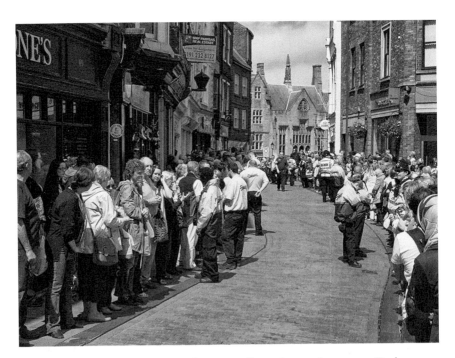

FIGURE 4.8 Security directing people as part of crowd control measures, Durham, Queen's Jubilee Parade, 2012

Source: © Teresa Leopold.

THINK POINT

Have you been to an event where a worker has influenced your experience or your performance? How was your experience influenced?

---

does not occur simply in the obvious places but can transform the meanings and uses of people, things, and ideas located far from bombs or camouflaged fatigues'. Certainly being aware of the meanings attached to what appears at first sight to be harmless fun can only aid understanding of the implications of such ventures on the social world. This process is also apparent in the context of events. For example, one UK-based events company organises environmental education programmes for their clients in which participants are required to dress in army camouflage and are subsequently 'put through their paces in boot camp style'. This process is also evident in Figure 4.9, which shows a military stand at an Olympic Torch Relay event in Wales in 2012.

The point in the examples referred to above is that, by having connections with the military, many social practices can be argued to be underscored with legitimised violence, if one accepts Enloe's approach.

FIGURE 4.9 Military stand during the Olympic Torch Relay, 2012

Source: © Hazel Andrews.

Spectators as part of the performance

Contextualising performances, which take place during events, is therefore important for gaining a clear picture of the meaning of an event. Thus, why and how people consume an event directs the meaning that they attach to the event itself and which therefore an event has. This raises the question of how and why people consume events, which will be explored in more detail in chapter 5. What we need to note within the context of performance, however, is that 'participants not only do things, they try to show others what they are doing or have done; actions take on a "performed-for-an-audience" aspect' (Schechner 1977, cited in Turner 1987: 4). This leads us back to the question posed at the beginning of the chapter, as to whether spectators are part of an event performance. Consider, for example the importance of chanting and singing during a football match. It is unnecessary to mention that the performance of spectators in a football stadium largely contributes to and directs the atmosphere of the event. The audience clearly becomes part of the performance. In general, it could be argued that individuals' performances, whether during active or passive scenarios, always have the potential to influence other people's experiences; for example, imagine you attend an opera performance and the person sitting next to you keeps coughing and blowing her/his nose. In this scenario, although your neighbour is also a passive member in the audience, the fact that she/he has a cold might still influence your event experience. Clearly, we need to acknowledge that event attendees' satisfaction with an event can be influenced by a number of factors, not just the performance of others. These include an individual's mood and well-being at the time of attendance, an individual's willingness to take part in activities that form part of an event, the actual stage performance of actors, the organisation of an event and the expectations that individuals have before an event.

Performance of and with event 'products'

So far we have drawn links between performance studies and events through a discussion of why consumers attend performances, which goes beyond pure motivational studies, and how different consumers participate in performances. Let us now turn our attention to how the event consumer performs with the event products, which aligns with Deighton's (1992) categories of 'consumers performing with products' and 'products performing for consumers. While we explore the notion of consumption in the event context in more detail in chapter 5, it is important to highlight some of the important debates regarding the performance of event products. Event products can range from the actual event experience to goods, such as merchandise, event memorabilia and food and drink, which contribute to making the event. Indeed a performance that takes place during an event can also be considered a product in itself or part of an event product. This can be illustrated by looking at the Bluff Oyster Festival in Southern New Zealand. Various event elements contribute to the actual event product, namely the festival itself. Thus, a key attraction of the festival is the food, mainly seafood and fish-related products, which can be purchased and tried once a festival visitor has entered the festival grounds. We can argue here that visitors perform with the food through a continuous purchasing and trying of different food products. In addition, various performances take place throughout the festival ranging from sea-related fashion shows to oyster-eating competitions. These performances not only form part of the overall event but present performances, which consumers can choose to engage with.

Products have long been approached as symbolic, which provides them with meanings beyond their functional values (Levy 1959, 1964, 1980 and Zaltman and Wallendorf 1979, in Solomon 1983: 319). To illustrate this within the event context, visitors of music concerts often have the opportunity to purchase products such as t-shirts and hats, which portray images or the name of the performer. The functional role of a hat for example might be to protect the wearer against the elements while the symbolic meaning might suggest the wearer has been to a concert and is a fan of the music artist. Even more, depending on the genre of music or the popularity of the artist at the time, the product might suggest that the wearer is cool or even that he/she belongs to a certain group of people. Similarly, Tenfelde (1978: 13) explores the important symbolic meaning of flags during mining celebrations:

> On such occasions ... flags played a special part. The flag was the visible expression of the Knappschaft [in this case, mining fraternity], of its unity, its exclusiveness, and its devotion to state and monarch. A flag, when it was not given by highly-placed personages or even mine-owners, was graciously granted by the king and presented to the Knappschaft as a mark of distinction. At a later date, miners, at some sacrifice to themselves, would subscribe from their own funds, sometimes over years, in order to obtain a flag for their associations.

In this case, we can argue that the flags perform by presenting a certain meaning for the mining community, but also for visitors of the festivals. Thus, when an event has simultaneous functions, products also perform and contain complex meanings ranging from being considered an important stream of income (Walo et al. 1996) to symbolic meaning or indeed functional value, such as a sunhat. The importance of certain products becomes apparent when the role they can play in rituals and ceremonies is considered. In such contexts certain products or memorabilia perform important functions without which the event would have less meaning.

THINK POINT

During an Olympic year, the Olympic Torch is lit in Athens and moved to the host country. It is then carried throughout different regions until it arrives at the Opening Ceremony to light the Olympic Flame. What is the meaning of the torch? What function does it perform?

Contested performances

Finally we want to turn our attention to the role of contested performances in the event context. In our introductory chapter we posed the question of whether acts of civil disobedience such as street battles and demonstrations can be considered events. These examples, with many other forms of social contestation, can be considered contested performances. To understand these expressions of resistance, often the underlying political significance and/or meaning of cultural movements need to be considered through a continued return to 'the nexus between culture and power' (Hall and Jefferson 2006: ix). At the same time, we have to consider that their size, impact and meaning often influence the attention they receive from the media and therefore from society at large. Hall and Jefferson's (2006: viii) study of 'resistance through rituals' focuses on the role of youth sub-cultures by arguing that 'spectacular youth subcultures raised questions about the necessarily contested and contradictory character of cultural change, and the diversity of forms in which such "resistances" might find expression'.

THINK POINT

Search the internet to find a range of different examples of events which you would consider as 'contested forms of expression'. Analyse them in more detail: How were they organised? What is their cultural meaning? What is their political significance?

One example that you could have found is the Tiananmen Square Demonstrations in Beijing, China, from April to June 1989. These mass demonstrations turned into a massacre and became a powerful symbol for economic change, freedom of the press and political liberalisation. This illustrates 'how performative such occasions become' (Allain and Harvie 2006: 117) where public spaces such as streets and squares form the stage for these acts. In addition, like other performances, contested events often display specific products and elements (such as signs, speeches or specific clothes, e.g. hoodies), which reflect the discussions above regarding the different approaches to the event product as performance. Acknowledging political significance and cultural meaning as attributes of contested events, many forms of events (such as carnivals) can be considered as or might include forms of social contestation. For example, Cohen (1982: 24) argues that:

> carnivals are generally a fertile field for exploring [identities of cultures], as their symbolic forms have the potentiality for political articulation, serving in some situations as 'rituals of rebellion', whose function is cathartic and is ultimately a mechanism helping in the maintenance of the established order; and in other situations as expressions of resistance, protest and violence.

In other words, different types of events can become contested due to planned or unplanned expressions of violence and resistance, which might take place, often without consideration for the actual reasons behind the social contestation. This is illustrated in the case study 'The degeneration of a "fan party" into a hooligan riot'.

CASE STUDY: THE DEGENERATION OF A 'FAN PARTY' INTO A 'HOOLIGAN RIOT'

Rangers Football Club of Glasgow played the UEFA Cup Final against Russian club Zenit St Petersburg in the City of Manchester Stadium in May 2008. Media reports about the football game focused largely on bad behaviour by Rangers fans, with 42 having been arrested. Rangers fans were largely blamed for the degeneration of a fan party into an act of hooliganism. While they had initially engaged in a socially acceptable performance, their behaviour had shifted to become a contested performance. Millward (2009) however provides an alternative view to that presented by the media, which reiterates the point that, in order to understand contested events, one has to look at and explore their underlying cultural movement, meaning and political significance. Five reasons are given which provide an explanation for the behaviour of Rangers fans during the match and counteract the mass-media representation of the incidents, which reflects many predetermined ideas regarding Rangers fans as being the 'worst behaved' football supporters (O'Neill 2005, cited in Millward 2009: 384).

Organisational difficulties, in addition to a lack of preparedness, were behind three key reasons for the way the event unfolded. First, the number of Rangers fans travelling to Manchester to watch the game was underestimated. This resulted in a challenging timeframe, in that Manchester City Council and Greater Manchester Police only had six days before the game to organise three fan zones in the city for 100,000 fans. Second, these fan zones were situated in Manchester city centre, which is already a busy area during the week (the game took place on a Wednesday). Third, large TV screens were put up in each fan zone, however, in the Piccadilly Gardens fan zone the TV screen was not working due to technical problems. Thus supporters were trying to leave the fan area to watch the game elsewhere, which resulted in a confrontation between the police and fans. The other two reasons presented by Millward refer to the intoxication of many fans, which influenced their behaviour and reactions to the technological failure of the TV screen. Finally, the measures used by police officers during the evening to deal with some fans being in an inebriated state were considered more excessive than during the day. Millward discusses fans being rounded up and knocked to the ground by the Tactical Support Group, while some fans who questioned the behaviour of the support group were hit with batons. This 'use of excessive force' was the subject of 38 out of a total of 63 complaints against the Greater Manchester Police.

(*Source*: Millward 2009)

Organisational challenges and mistakes, intoxication and misbehaviour by fans and the police resulted in the social disorder that made this UEFA Cup Final such a contested event. Of particular interest in this case study is the role of the media, in that it gave a very contested and one-sided perception of the events, which in turn influenced social perceptions. This will be further discussed in chapter 6.

Summary

In this chapter we explored:

- the idea of the event as a performance and the different roles involved;
- the difference between social and cultural performances;
- the importance of the context in understanding and shaping events as performances;
- the role of products and their symbolic significance in the performance of events;
- the nature of contested performances and their role within the event context.

Suggested reading

Deighton, J. (1992) 'The Consumption of Performance', *Journal of Consumer Research*, 19(3): 362–72.

Goffman, E. (1959) *The Presentation of the Self in Everyday Life*. Harmondsworth: Penguin.

Hall, S. and Jefferson, T. (2006) *Resistance through Rituals: Youth Subcultures in Post-War Britain*. London: Routledge.

Schechner, R. (2003) *Performance Theory*. New York: Routledge.

Schechner, R. (2006) *Performance Studies*. New York: Routledge.

Useful websites

British and International Federation of Festivals: http://www.federationoffestivals.org.uk
Royal Wedding: http://www.officialroyalwedding2011.org
Halloween: http://www.novareinna.com/festive/hallow.html
Bluff Oyster Festival: http://www.bluffoysterfest.co.nz
Nice Carnival: http://www.nicecarnaval.com
Notting Hill Carnival: http://www.thenottinghillcarnival.com

5

EVENTS AND CONSUMPTION

In this chapter we explore the relationship between events and consumer society in more detail. We examine definitions of some key terms relating to consumption practices and consumer society and how these relate to the experience economy. In addition we also consider issues relating to the commodification of culture and what this says about authenticity. By thinking about the meanings attributed to objects and practices of consumption we will also be able to examine questions of identity and lifestyle and reflect on social class and social inclusion and exclusion. We will also note that not all events are concerned with consuming but those based around charities are concerned with encouraging people to give. With this in mind we will consider the idea of conspicuous giving. The main points of this chapter are:

- to define consumption;
- to discuss commodification and authenticity;
- to link consumption practices and identity;
- to understand conspicuous giving.

Consumption

When we use the term 'consumption' we need to be clear about what we mean. We may think about it in terms of using something or eating something and so its meaning appears quite straightforward. However, the term 'consumption' is quite problematic because it is often treated differently across academic disciplines and even within the same discipline (Bocock 1993). When looking for the meaning of a concept, as we have seen in previous chapters, starting with a dictionary definition is often useful so that we can trace the development of a word. In this respect the *Shorter Oxford English Dictionary* (*SOED*) definition offers four interpretations of consumption:

1. The act or fact of consuming by use, waste etc.
2. Decay, wasting away, or wearing out; waste
3. Wasting of the body by disease; a wasting disease; now applied spec. to pulmonary consumption
4. *Pol. Econ.* The destructive employment of industrial products; the amount of them consumed.

The *SOED* definition has an emphasis on waste and destruction that implies an end point to something's use value. The problem with this is that even if it were possible to identify an end point that in itself would be the subject of interpretation by different users. As Jackson (1993: 209) asks 'how many times can we listen to a cassette tape or compact disk before it is fully consumed?'

In many discussions of consumption it appears to be taken as read that it involves the purchase of a commodity or commodities, and, as such, understandings of consumption have been largely within the canon of economics. This is related to the processes of modernisation referred to in chapter 2. During the late seventeenth century and early eighteenth century the domestic consumer market expanded, which led to the need to understand consumption's place within the economic cycle. It was related to the income of the consumer, seen as a function of production, and discussed in purely quantitative terms (Friedman 1994). Viewing consumption in this way is a limited conceptualisation that reduces the practice to 'a momentary act of purchase' (Jackson 1993: 208).

THINK POINT

Compare websites for different types of events, for example, carnival, music concerts, sporting events, food markets and religious events. What kind of products are advertised for people to consume? How much importance is given to the consumable items as being part of the event? What are the links between the products and the event?

An example website which you might have looked at is the Olympic Games 2012 merchandise website (the web link is provided at the end of this chapter). Figure 5.1 shows some of the products that have been produced for people to consume as part of the London Olympics in 2012. In the photograph we can see products ranging from dolls to t-shirts, most of which are associated with the two mascots of the Games, Wenlock and Mandeville.

The narrowness of economic definitions of consumption has been challenged and as a result consumption has been considered in terms of broader meanings. In other words, rather than just seeing an event as a product, which is available for consumption, there is the need to consider it as a product whose consumption has meaning and takes place in a social context (Robinson *et al.* 2004). It has been

FIGURE 5.1 Merchandise for the London Olympics, 2012

Source: © Hazel Andrews

suggested that the interest of social scientists in the study of consumption has in part developed beyond the canon of economic concerns. This in turn has given rise to its own problems; as Miller (1995: 283) points out, consumption 'has rapidly expanded to mean anything from the popular appropriation of state services to the literal translation of ingestion in traditional Hinduism'. However, moving away from an understanding of consumption in purely economic terms allows us to think more carefully about what the goods and services we might consume mean, and that it is possible to think about the demand for goods beyond being solely equated with price. Rather, goods have a symbolic value and lived associations. The photograph in Figure 5.2 was taken in the morning of St Patrick's Day in Dublin

FIGURE 5.2 Beer kegs for St Patrick's Day in Dublin, 2010

Source: © Teresa Leopold

and shows the large number of beer kegs that were delivered to a pub. Looking at the picture, we could just analyse it from an economic exchange perspective, in that people purchase beer as part of the festival. However, we could also question the meaning of beer consumption, and particularly consumption of Guinness, during the festival.

THINK POINT

Think about past events that you have attended. What did you consume at the events? Why did you consume/purchase it?

Kates (2003: 6) highlights the complexity, importance and different forms of consumption in his discussion of the Sydney Gay and Lesbian Mardi Gras:

> In 1978, the Mardi Gras started as a street protest of approximately 1,500 people; during this protest, the Sydney police attacked the 'rioting mob' and arrested 53 of them (Carbery 1995). In fewer than 20 years, however, the festival has developed into one in which hundreds of thousands of consumers eat, drink, watch the parade, dress up, shop, dance, and participate in many other consumption events such as film nights and the 'infamous' Mardi Gras party which follows the parade itself.

Goods and objects consumed during this festival, such as dresses worn, are ascribed meanings, so that 'for one day at least, gender conventions and "natural" standards of decency, masculinity, and femininity were fair game for exaggeration, profanation, and play' (Kates 2003: 11). It is not just a dress that someone might wear but often a statement that the wearer is making, so that objects and things go beyond their pure function to *mean* something. In relation to events we can see the importance and meaning of things in Charlotte Hagström's study of christening gifts in Sweden (see case study 'To create a sense of belongings – christening gifts as materialisation of feelings).

CASE STUDY: TO CREATE A SENSE OF BELONGINGS – CHRISTENING GIFTS AS MATERIALISATION OF FEELINGS

Hagström notes that giving presents at christenings is an old tradition. The sorts of gifts given include money boxes, jewellery, clothes, toys, money, photo albums and silver spoons. However, most of these items will be meaningless to the baby concerned, given that most christenings take place when a baby is a few months old. For her research Hagström was concerned with finding out what was important about these items for this particular event. The recurring theme that she found was based on relations: the presents given had often been in a family for several generations or were linked to a place of importance, for example where a family originated from. The objects were also often linked to the giver – an aunt, grandparent or family friend. The things therefore represented family and friendship ties; as Hagström (2007: 143) says: 'through these things people were linked together and relations between them were expressed and manifest[ed]'. Some presents given for christenings can be used at the time of their giving, others require the child concerned to grow up. An example of this type of present is the coffee spoon. The spoon would not be of immediate use to a young baby but, by giving the utensil, the giver is indicating that the relation between the giver and receiver will extend into the future, to a point when the child will be able to use the coffee spoon. The giving of silver tableware is not an unusual present but it can be expensive. Hagström reports on a jeweller's advertisement aimed at encouraging grandparents to collect silverware for their grandchildren so that, by the time they reach maturity, they will have a full set of cutlery to use in their own home. The table silver therefore becomes a link between past and future and, when utilised, it links the present to the past. Hagström's (2007:146) final remarks make the overall point very well:

> Christening gifts are on the one hand very concrete and material. They have a value, both economically and emotionally. But on the other hand they also have a function that is neither concrete nor material. They express feelings, hopes, and dreams of belonging and community. The gift has a meaning for both the one who receives it, and the one who presents the gift.

(*Source*: Hagström 2007)

It is these meanings that link consumption practices with the reproduction of identity and social relations. Before we connect consumption choices to these two areas of social life we need to consider the issue of commodification.

Commodification

Kevin Meethan (2001: 5) sums up the meaning of commodification quite nicely when he states it is 'the ways in which material culture, people and places become objectified for the purposes of the global market'. What Meethan is referring to is the ways by which things, people and places become commodities. A commodity is an item that has had a price attached to it and can be bought and sold. Thus the food we buy, our clothes and our household items – fridges, TVs, furniture and so on – are all commodities. Turning things into commodities is part of consumer cultures so that, within the context of events, we can see many cultural festivals and rituals being repackaged as commodities. One example is when Pope Benedict visited Bavaria in 2006. This religious event was commodified, with a huge range of merchandise and goods available to celebrate the event ranging from 'Papst-Bier' (pope beer) to Vatican flags, mugs and beer glasses with pictures of the Pope, and specific websites dedicated to promoting the visit. Another example can be seen in Figure 5.3, which shows a café advertising food as part of the Queen's Jubilee celebrations in the UK in 2012.

Turning things into commodities does not only refer to the actual cultural goods that are produced and consumed, such as songs, food and dances, but also to experiences. Indeed, *experiencing* festivals and cultural events, and even the 'fantasy of an imagined and desired experience' of an event, presents a commodity (Green 2007: 205).

What needs to be remembered within this context is that when events become objectified and commodified, there is the need to differentiate one event from the other. Thus, many commodified events (such as the Trinidad Carnival (Green 2007)) represent certain cultural elements while disregarding others, so that the authenticity of such events may get lost (this will be explored in more detail below). Such a commodification process might impact on local and regional relationships, and local and personal identities. A different viewpoint is presented by Phipps (2011: 120), in his work on an Indigenous cultural festival in Australia. While acknowledging the danger of commodification of cultural elements, he argues that: 'cultural festivals at very least provide opportunities for direct encounters with Indigenous people that can counteract some of the routine colonising practices'. In other words, the consumption and commodification of indigenous values, customs, games, music and dances presents the possibility for 'serious, joyful and urgent acts of cultural politics'.

In terms of events, we can see that many festivals and rituals that were once of local interest become part of the package of entertainment for tourists, something the tourists pay to see, either indirectly because they have bought a holiday at a particular destination in which an event is held, or directly by paying, where required, either to participate in or view such events. It is this interest by tourists in such activities, as part of the sightseeing of touristic practice, that has contributed to what Boissevain has described as the revitalisation of European rituals (in addition to the rise of secularism, an increase in diasporic populations, increased democratisation and mobility). He comments in relation to Malta:

Religious and secular public celebrations attract tourists. These visitors are generally welcomed. The expertise of the organizers and, ultimately, the prestige of the celebrating community, are generally gauged by the size of the audience and the media attention the celebration attracts. National and local

FIGURE 5.3 Café advertising special food products, Queen's Jubilee, UK, 2012

Source: © Hazel Andrews.

tourist authorities have consequently actively promoted popular festivities. They have enlarged traditional feasts, have reintroduced events no longer celebrated and even invented new celebrations.

(Boissevain 2008: 28)

THINK POINT

There are famous festivals, carnivals and celebrations around the globe that attract international tourists. List as many as you can. Think about your own holiday experiences and identify your awareness of attendance at local events, again listing what they were.

That local activities or events become commodified and objects of the tourist gaze is problematic. Davydd Greenwood's (1989) influential and controversial paper about the Alarde ritual in the Basque community of Fuenterrabia, Spain set the tone for much of the academic debate that followed about making people and places into commodities for the benefit of tourists and tourism. The festival that Greenwood discusses was promoted to tourists by the Spanish tourism ministry and private companies. As the parade became very popular, the local authority said that it should take place twice on the same day to enable as many people as possible to see it. Greenwood (1989: 179) argued that the festival lost its meaning as it was no longer just performed for local people but became a show for outsiders; that thereby the culture was being sold 'by the pound' and as such the people were being robbed 'of the very meanings by which they organise their lives'. This argument has since been criticised as too general, and counter-arguments that suggest that the involvement of tourists helps to revitalise local customs have since been made. As Abram (1996: 46) points out in connection to rural events in the Auvergne region of France, there is no 'simple "effect of tourism" . . . tourism of some sorts may enhance local social activity by providing the audience required to frame a performance'.

The debate about the commodification of culture brings us to a related idea, that of authenticity. Quite simply 'authenticity' refers to that which is genuine and real, not fake. We have to consider different aspects when discussing authenticity and events. First, accepting the viewpoint that events are cultural commodities, authenticity can be considered as adding economic value to a cultural product (such as a cultural event or carnival) (Green 2007). In other words, by choosing to present specific authentic event elements the attractiveness of the event increases, which might then influence its economic value. For example, consider a *regional organic* food festival. The products sold are not just considered to be plain consumable food items but authentic products, that is, they are from the region and produced under organic conditions. Thus, by having an event, which focuses on *regional organic* produce, the authenticity of the products results in an enhanced value of the event commodity for the consumers.

Second, event organisers choose certain elements of an event over others and, by making this decision, they give greater authenticity to these elements. Thus, by making the decision to present a certain element as part of an event, it gains value in the eyes of visitors and attendees (Green 2007: 204): 'Cultural nationalists, in seeking to solidify national culture, authenticate some forms over others. These authenticated cultural forms are then incorporated within economic development schemes as representative of the nation. The authentication process freezes the dynamism of national culture.'

CASE STUDY: INTERNATIONAL FESTIVAL OF THE SEA

Bristol hosted the International Festival of the Sea in 1996 to celebrate the city's naval maritime history and heritage. The large-scale event attracted over 360,000 people and was broadcast on TV. However, decisions were made in the run-up to the event to present certain elements of Bristol's heritage, such as its 'supposedly proud, seafaring, maritime history' (Atkinson and Laurier 1998: 200), while ignoring the city's role in the slave trade and imperialism. On the one hand, this led to generally positive elements of Bristol's history being presented as a true representation of the city's past. On the other hand, choosing to ignore contested issues such as slavery made these issues 'disappear', so that tourists could not consume them and these elements were thus given no authentic value or importance in the event and the city's history. In addition, two traveller camps, which were situated close to the festival site were evicted to ensure the 'fantasy identity' (Atkinson and Laurier 1998: 200) of the city for tourists. Thus, the setting was sanitised by removing people, who did not fit into the desired image of the city.

(*Source*: Atkinson and Laurier 1998)

However, at the same time that local people feel that their traditions and way of life are being overly commodified, and either losing meaning or developing a meaning people are uncomfortable with, they will seek ways to change the terms by which they engage with such activities. Jeremy Boissevain (2008, drawing on Dekker 1993) again provides a good example. In the Dutch village of Holten, Easter is celebrated with neighbourhood bonfires. The local authorities decided that, in order to increase the attractiveness of the event to tourists, they would organise one very large bonfire. Local people were unhappy with this development and simply ignored it, continuing to organise the more localised events. The question that a visitor might ask is: to what extent is the organised or staged bonfire 'authentic', and are the genuine celebrations to be found with the neighbourhood bonfires?

A final link between authenticity and events refers to the idea of 'front' and 'back' regions. This is based on the work of Erving Goffman (1959), who argues that we present a self to the world as if we are engaged in a performance in a similar way to actors in a theatre, but that, 'behind the scenes' so to speak, is the true self. This argument has been widely explored in the tourism studies literature (see for example MacCannell 1976; Boissevain 1996) and can also be applied to the event context in that events are 'front' stages, and thus platforms where certain cultural elements are presented as authentic to potential consumers, while 'back' stages are protected for locals. It is sometimes the case that 'staged events' are used to avoid intrusion into the authentic, perhaps more private domain, by visitors and onlookers. In some cases non-locals are excluded altogether. For example, Poppi (1992) studies celebrations in the village of Penia, Val di Fassa Valley, Italy. During the carnival tourists were banned from parts of the valley to ensure that the event was for 'insiders' only. It has been argued that, in their search for something real and more genuine, tourists attempt to penetrate into these secluded and private back areas even more. The question for event managers is how to balance the privacy of local inhabitants with that of commercial interests and the satisfaction of interested outsiders.

These arguments, which link authenticity to events, reflect much debate in the tourism studies literature (see 'Suggested reading' at the end of the chapter to find some good starting points if you would like to explore these issues further). As discussed in this section, the processes of commodification and elements of 'authenticity' influence the meaning of events and event products, and hence our consumption practices in relation to them. We will now discuss how these meanings link consumption practices with the reproduction of identity and social relations.

Consumption and identity

One of the first works to be written about consumption is Thorstein Veblen's (1925 [1899]) *A Theory of the Leisure Class*. His main argument is that class divisions can be identified by the ability to 'waste time', by which he means using time not spent in productive labour, working in a factory or in agriculture, etc. At the same time, the 'leisure class' were also able to buy goods beyond their 'basic needs' of food, clothes and shelter. For example, women in the leisure class that Veblen identified dressed in a certain style, which restricted their movements, indicating that they were not engaged in the working practices of women of lower classes that required greater bodily movement. Thus the different styles of dresses became markers of the class to which the women belonged.

Similar ideas were developed by Pierre Bourdieu (1979). In his famous book *Distinction* he showed that people's consumption practices are indicative of class divisions. In this respect, all items of culture can be used as a means of expression of the self, and thus, as a mark of difference from somebody else. What this tells us is that we express ideas and feelings through objects and things.

Bourdieu was concerned with how our consumption patterns relate to notions of self-identity and serve to reinforce that identity. He rejects narrow economic definitions of social relations, arguing that capital is not solely based in economic monetary terms but is also evident in the tastes expressed by a person, finding its form in, for example, art, food and drink. The class '*habitus*' of the individual, which they are born into in terms of the social structures (age, ethnicity, education, etc.), social positions (one's social, economic and cultural capital) and the social milieu (which shapes an individual's values and aims) governs one's tastes, behaviours, preferences, likes and dislikes.

THINK POINT

Note down five statements/words that describe your personal background, interests, family situation or surroundings. For example: I come from a close and big family, I am not very religious, I am interested in sports and outdoors, I enjoy learning about new cultures and meeting new people, etc.

Reflect on and think about your statements by addressing some of the following questions: Why do you believe it? Why are you interested in . . . ? How does this influence your life? Has this influenced your choice of study – why and how so? How important is it to you? Why is it important to you?

Consumer items are used as marks of distinction with regard to occupational and class divisions, and their consumption is part of the process of communicating that identity. In turn, such consumption practices will reinforce the identity of that class. 'Taste classifies, and it classifies the classifier. Social subjects classified by their classifications, distinguish themselves by the distinctions they make' (Bourdieu 1979: 6). Among others, one question which emerges from a discussion of notions of consumption and identity within the event context is: how does our identity influence the consumption of an event?

To answer this question, we can draw links between consumption processes, identity and the event context. Building on Fortier's (1999) argument that identity is formed by people's sense of belonging to a certain place, Duffy (2009) focuses her discussion of the communal Brunswick Music Festival in Australia and how it is defined as a multicultural event to represent local people's feelings of belonging, notions of individual identity but also communal identity. In other words, the multicultural community of Brunswick is represented through a multicultural music festival. There are two important points to note here: first, the festival is performed and consumed as a multicultural festival, which represents locals' identities; and, second, the festival is not only consumed but simultaneously a communal multicultural identity is produced. In such a communal event identity is dynamic in that it is constantly re-formed through new, shared experiences and memories of old experiences (Costa 2002).

However, we have to remember that the communication of identity through goods (used here to mean not only material objects but also colour schemes, styles and designs) and represented in events serves not just as a statement of who one is, but also of who one is not. This argument has been explored by Mary Douglas (1996: 104) who asserts that the choices exercised over purchases of clothes, cosmetics and in hairstyles, toothpastes, etc. demonstrate that 'shopping is an agonistic struggle to define not what one is, but what one is not'. In this respect consumption practices can be seen as activities of resistance. Thus, choosing to engage in some events and not in others not only tells us about the identity being confirmed but also what types of identity we reject.

THINK POINT

Would everyone see him or herself as comfortable at a Goth music festival or going to a performance at the Royal Opera House in London's Covent Garden? Explain the answer.

The final point that we would like to discuss in terms of identity and consumption is the idea that consumption practices reflect class or lifestyle. Bourdieu's emphasis on class identity is problematic in that the terms 'working', 'middle' and 'upper' class have been rejected by some in the so-called postmodern world in favour of the term 'lifestyle' (Bocock 1993). One definition of lifestyle argues that it involves 'individuality, self-expression, and stylistic self-consciousness. One's body, clothes, speech, leisure pastimes, eating and drinking preferences, home, car, choice of holidays, etc. are to be regarded as indicators of the individuality of taste and sense of style of the owner/consumer' (Featherstone 1991: 83). In this definition, lifestyle is still a communication of identity, which in part relies on consumption practices, and, further, those lifestyles acted out or aspired to still serve to create a form of social stratification. In addition, the behaviour attached to particular lifestyles can still be used, as Douglas (1996) identifies, as a means by which the definition of self and other is created.

The accent on individuality and the self inherent in the use of the term 'lifestyle' misses the potential for shared social experiences and opportunities for the creation of social solidarity. Thus not only should the study of consumption practices be concerned with individual identities (as illustrated in the case study below), but also how they allow common identities to be established (Longhurst and Savage 1996; Warde 1996).

CASE STUDY: WEDDING MARKETS – SEASONS FOR SALE

Knuts (2007: 148) discusses how the market is intertwined with wedding rituals to the extent that they 'are amplifying each other', and claims that 'the time, money and energy that people, in today's Swedish society, put into their weddings are increasing' (2007: 149). Furthermore, bigger and more lavish weddings have become 'standard', in part due to higher incomes, and access to funds in the form of loans and credit cards, and it has become more common to take out loans to pay for expensive weddings. Such practices form part of consumer culture. Overall weddings are 'big business'. A report in a Swedish newspaper in 2004 noted that the wedding industry had an estimated yearly turnover of 3.5 billion Swedish kronor (SEK) or about €30 million. This did not include expenditure by guests on gifts, new clothes and travel but these would probably account for an additional SEK 1.5 billion.

Knuts points out that in order to get married we do not need many of the objects we associate with the occasion – special clothes, rings, flowers – and yet these material things, along with many other aspects of materiality are an important part of getting married for many people. The objects that we include in getting married are commodities. On the one hand they are things that are bought and sold but on the other they also convey messages about love and romance. In this respect by making commodities of the things that represent our feelings the feelings are in turn commodified.

Knuts explores the process of getting married by identifying the planning or timeline that leads up to the ritual or event itself. This is often accompanied by a wedding planning calendar which outlines the plan of the wedding in increasing detail as the date approaches. Thus it begins with 12 months before 'set the date' and moves to 'decide a theme' (10 months before) and 'look for a dress' (6 months before). People planning a wedding can choose from a range of commodities, styles and themes. 'There are thousands of dresses to choose from, thousands of bouquets, thousands of hairstyles, thousands of menus' (Knuts 2007: 150). Distinctiveness is therefore an important element of an individual's wedding. Thus, while it is recognised that a wedding requires certain things to make it a wedding, it is important that it is personalised in order for it to be 'something special'. In order to help the wedding planner cope with the amount of choice available Knuts notes that wedding magazines have developed 'packages' based on the style of wedding required, for example 'romantic', 'elegant', 'different'. The season in which the wedding takes place has also become part of the package in terms of thinking about the seasonality of food, weather and scenic background available at different times of the year, although the main wedding season is Whitsun to August. Reasons for not getting married at the most popular wedding time are that it makes it more distinctive, will be less costly and easier to organise.

(*Source*: Knuts 2007)

In the academic discussions about lifestyle and class there are debates about whether lifestyle has necessarily replaced class categories. The post-Fordist world and its connection to the idea of postmodernism explored in chapter 2 is argued to have led to the emergence of new middle classes (not one middle class but *classes*), which is connected to growth in media (advertising, lifestyle research), caring, personal services (acupuncture, reflexology) and the emergence of a service-based economy more generally.

To be clear on the point (regardless of whether lifestyle or class is used to determine what is being communicated), acts of consumption operate to convey notions of identity to self and others, and are used to create social relations, facilitating a sense of social solidarity. However, research and discussion of consumption practices in the last few years, particularly within business contexts such as marketing and events management, has embraced the notion of *experience* as fundamental to consumer decisions. This will be explored in the next section of this chapter.

Changes in consumption practice

Holbrook and Hirschman (1982: 132) were among the first to introduce the 'experiential view' into the discussion of consumption practices by arguing: 'Consumption has begun to be seen as involving a steady flow of fantasies, feelings, and fun encompassed by what we call the "experiential view".' This notion was further developed within the economic context by Pine and Gilmore (1998) so that nowadays consumption practices are considered to have changed from being purely *functional* to satisfy one's needs (e.g. attending a food market to purely purchase food) to being *memorable* through the creation of experiences (e.g. attending a food market to experience the atmosphere or gain a feeling of satisfaction by supporting local farmers). In other words, consumers are now searching for experiences to satisfy their needs so that consumer studies now consider experiences as being crucial within consumer decision making.

However, what does the term 'experience' actually mean? Carú and Cova (2003: 269) stress that experience has now become an 'all-embracing term, which is often used to indicate some experience that a person has in everyday life', and discuss the different disciplinary meanings of the term such as personal trials (philosophy), a subjective and cognitive activity (sociology and psychology) and an experiment (science). Thus, they are highlighting the challenging context, which arises from the difficulty of defining the word. Andrews (2009) also explores the complexities around the meaning of experience in relation to the context of tourism, which, she argues, can be understood as an event.

THINK POINT

Define the word 'experience' in your own words.

Within the context of events management, experience is often seen as something that, on the one hand can be created through good planning and management. and on the other needs to be co-created by consumers. This reflects Pine and Gilmore's

(1999) argument that organisations need to create unique and memorable experiences, or the fantasy of such, to ensure that they gain an advantage to their competitors. Understanding the consumer thus becomes crucial.

Morgan *et al.* (2009: 203) discuss three emerging themes of consumer experience, which also apply to the event context:

1 'a shift of emphasis from the rational to the emotional aspects of consumer decision making', in that consumers now make decisions not only based on service or product attributes but also emotional elements such as feelings, escapism, entertainment and novelty (e.g. attending a home show for entertainment reasons rather than to become aware of a new product base);
2 'a transition from satisfying needs to fulfilling aspirations, desires and dreams'. This reflects our discussion above that consumption and the products that we choose to consume present meaning and become part of one's identity (e.g. partaking in a community festival to have a shared experience and feel part of the community);
3 'the role of the customer as an active participant rather than a passive consumer', so that consumers become co-creators of their experiences. Consumers' motivations to attend an event play a role within this context in that the reason for attending an event can determine how they experience and become involved in an event, that is, whether they are passive consumers or active participants. For example, a family might attend a football game to foster family togetherness, while someone else might go to support the team. Both would be active participants and co-creators in the experience (one through fostering family togetherness and the other by supporting their team) though their level of immersion in the event might differ.

THINK POINT

Think of different event examples for each of the three themes of consumer experience discussed above.

Within this discussion we need to recognise that the consumption experience such as attending and experiencing an event involves different stages, which go beyond the actual consumption of the product. Arnould *et al.* (2002, cited in Carú and Cova 2003: 269) highlight four stages of consumption experience, which reminds us of Clawson and Knetsch's (1966) three-stage experience model of outdoor recreation (anticipation, experience, recollection). Both approaches can be aligned to the event context as highlighted below:

• pre-consumption experience, for example, searching for, dreaming about and planning to attend an event;

- purchase experience, for example, purchase of or payment for event ticket, accommodation or specific dress;
- core consumption experience: actual event attendance, including feelings and emotions which arise during the experience;
- remembered consumption experience: recollection, memory and storytelling of the event experience.

All four stages influence consumers' experiences.

Thus far we have concentrated on consumption practices and activities. However, there are many events that are organised to encourage giving. This relates to fundraising activities for charities and good causes and is the subject of the next section.

Conspicuous giving

We have already noted the work of Veblen (1925 [1899]) in relation to goods being markers of class identity. As part of his work Veblen also developed the idea of 'conspicuous consumption'. This refers to the idea that money is spent on goods and services in order to display wealth and status. However, not all activities are based on consumption. Many events are organised for people to give. Filo *et al.* (2009) comment on the rise in charitable giving in the United States, which has been mirrored in rise in popularity of charity sport events. Indeed they note that many charities have recognised the value of charity sport events to raise funds, with the American Cancer Society's Relay of Life being the most successful charity sport event, raising over $350 million in 2006.

THINK POINT

List as many charity fundraising activities as you can. Think about what local organisations do to raise money. Think about national fundraising activities.

There are many reasons why people give to charities and good causes. It could be based on the simple desire to support an activity, to mark gratitude and support for the work of a cause (as is often the case following the death of a friend or relative people are asked to make donations to a charity rather than buy funeral flowers). The research by Filo *et al.*(2009) also highlighted three further main themes: (1) *camaraderie*, based around ideas of social solidarity, belonging and friendship; (2) *cause*, which is linked to the desire to do good and to both find inspiration and inspire others and (3) *competence*, based on preparation for and participation in the sporting event that links to ideas of health and fitness.

From a different perspective Cunningham *et al.* (2009: 65) note the importance of sponsorship for event organisations: 'International Events Group Network (IEG

Inc., 2005) has asserted that corporate sponsorship is the world's fastest growing marketing tool.' Drawing on the work of Kover (2001), they state that 'identifying any large scale or public event sans sponsorship is virtually impossible', noting that in 2007 worldwide spending on sponsorship was worth $38 billion.

THINK POINT

List as many corporate sponsors as you can. Who and what activities are being supported?

As might be expected the commercial reasons for sponsorship are linked to promotion of products or brands and Cunningham *et al.*(2009) explore in depth other business rationales and practices related to corporate sponsorship. However, besides these functional and practical considerations social scientists seek to understand the more complex associations with ideas of giving, some of which have been identified in the research by Filo *et al.* (2009). This is what brings us to the term 'conspicuous giving'.

Glazer and Konrad (1996) develop this term based on a series of quite complex mathematical formulae. They argue that the basis of charitable giving is to demonstrate wealth, and this works as 'signals' to those who cannot observe the commodities that we would normally associate with displays of wealth, for example a large house. The case study 'Princess Beatrice's hat' illustrates this point.

CASE STUDY: PRINCESS BEATRICE'S HAT

Following the wedding of Prince William to Katherine Middleton in April 2011 Prince William's cousin Princess Beatrice decided to auction her hat on ebay to raise funds for UNICEF and Children in Crisis. The hat, designed by Philip Treacy, had already received a lot of attention due to its unusual style. It eventually sold to an anonymous bidder for over £80,000, but not before interest had been expressed by a number of celebrities including, among others, Victoria Beckham, Cat Deeley and The Wiggles (Australian children's entertainers).

(*Source:* http://www.looktothestars.org/news/6329-celebrities-bid-on-royal-wedding-hat-for-charity)

The ability to give away a designer hat and for others to then enter into a bidding war are examples of conspicuous giving. This is not to say that the intentions behind donating the hat or bidding for it were completely without philanthropic reasons, although Glazer and Konrad (1996: 1021) claim that 'individuals who donate to signal their income will not make anonymous donations'. The majority of us will never be able to see into the private life of Princess Beatrice and therefore view the objects that demonstrate her privileged and wealthy background, but we can all learn about the hat.

The example of Princess Beatrice's hat is one that has a high public profile, yet similar arguments about conspicuous giving can also be applied to more 'everyday' charitable occasions. Glazer and Konrad (1996: 1024) found people were willing to give money to charities and good causes even if there was no increase in the 'provision of public good'. They argue that one of the motives is to be seen to be giving. For example, in the United States in 1991 universities received donations worth $10.2 billion of which $5 billion came from individuals and $2.3 billion from alumni. The listing of donations by alumni in university publicity and news materials can serve the purpose of signalling wealth to one's former peer group. The overall point being that the organisation of activities to raise money for charities and good causes is a way of mediating giving, and that making a spectacle of such activities enables the groups or individuals concerned to communicate something about themselves in the social world.

Summary

In this chapter we explored:

- the definition of consumption and the development of its meaning;
- the relationship between events and consumption activities and the use of commodities;
- how the commodification process has impacted on various types of events;
- the commodification of charitable giving.

Suggested reading

Atkinson, D. and Laurier, E. (1998) 'A Sanitised City? Social Exclusion at Bristol's 1996 International Festival of the Sea', *Geoforum*, 29(2): 199–206.

Carú, A. and Cova, B. (2003) 'Revisiting Consumption Experience: A More Humble But Complete View of the Concept', *Marketing Theory*, 3: 267–86.

Glazer, A. and Konrad, K. (1996) 'A Signaling Explanation for Charity', *American Economic Review*, 86(4): 1019–28.

Meethan, K. (2001) *Tourism and Global Society*. Basingstoke: Palgrave.

Useful websites

Sydney Mardi Gras: http://www.mardigras.org.au

Food Lovers Britain: http://www.foodloversbritain.com/foodevents

Look to the Stars: http://www.looktothestars.org/news/6329-celebrities-bid-on-royal-wedding-hat-for-charity

Olympic Merchandise: http://shop.london2012.com
Collaborative Consumption: http://www.collaborativeconsumption.com
Institute of Fundraising: http://www.institute-of-fundraising.org.uk/home
Information on Non-Profit Organisations: http://nonprofit.about.com
A greener festival: http://www.agreenerfestival.com

6

PLACE AND REPRESENTATION

In our introduction we emphasised that an event is a mix of elements that all overlap to inform the practice of an event. To remind you: we argued that events bring together elements of place, they involve people of different socio-cultural backgrounds and incorporate elements of business practices. It is to the first element, the issue of place that we now wish to turn. Thus, this chapter will introduce you to:

- ideas of place and landscape
- a sense of place and belonging
- how space is produced
- the role of media in constructing places and people.

The concepts of place and space have been widely discussed in different disciplines such as geography, and particularly human geography, social anthropology, media and cultural studies, and sociology. A discussion of place and space however needs to be embedded within a wider discussion of related concepts to provide a broader understanding of their importance in the studies of events. In this chapter we will first turn our attention to issues of place and landscape, while space will be discussed in more detail in our section on the production of space. Thus, although our main focus in this chapter will remain on issues of place we situate it within cultural processes and thus link it to the notion of landscape (Hirsch and O'Hanlon 1995), sense of place and belonging, as well as the production of space (Lefebvre 1991). We will draw necessary links to issues explored in earlier chapters, such as the idea of insider versus outsider perspectives, as discussed within the context of authenticity, the commodification of place, the role of experience in the perception of place and space, and the importance of performance in place and space production.

Place

The terms 'space' and 'place' are common words; we use them on a daily basis so that they represent 'basic components of the lived world' (Tuan 1977: 3). The feeling of home, of safety, attachment and meaning, is often linked to a certain *place*, for example, our apartment or our hometown. Thus place can be defined as a 'specific location' or even a 'portion of space designated or available for or being used by someone' (*Oxford English Dictionary*). However, these approaches do not recognise a more complex understanding of place. For the context of the study of events, we can turn to the field of tourism studies and adapt Pearce's (1995) explanation for place by arguing that events are about people and places (as also illustrated in Figure 1.1, chapter 1) in that people visit a specific place to encounter or take part in a happening. In other words, place is formed through relationships that people have to locations (whether they are familiar or not) and the meanings that develop through the interaction of location and people. So, rather than approaching place as a geographic location only, we need to think about how places are constructed and the meanings that they both retain and encourage to be developed through social relations, meaning and memory. Social interactions also occur in places in which events happen, so that meanings of events are created through shared practices and understandings in a certain place (Crouch 1999). 'Festivals [and other forms of events] thus provide unique opportunities to bring unrelated people together in novel ways . . . but also reinforce pre-existing relationships and social ties' (Gibson *et al.* 2011: 8).

THINK POINT

List examples of events which encourage strangers to interact with each other. List examples of events which encourage people who know each other to interact with each other.

Reflecting on the think point, you might have listed the same event in both sections. Consider for example a community event in a suburb or village. On the one hand such an event would encourage locals to meet with friends and neighbours from the village and thus reinforce pre-existing social relationships, while on the other hand it would also enable visitors and newcomers to the area to develop social ties. Thus, the event contributes to the development and production of a place by encouraging action and interaction of different people.

Globalisation, mass communication technology and increased mobility have been considered as challenging the understanding of place by encouraging a certain sense of placelessness. This means that places become interchangeable; they lack unique features so that the actual landscape and design of places replicate each other (e.g. airports, shopping centres) (Henderson 2009). At the same time, placelessness has been considered as providing a certain sense of freedom and liberation from otherwise structured and ordered places (Henderson 2009).

Thus, with the growth of mass communication some of our social interactions no longer take place in a specific geographic locale. Also, the development of online technology such as Skype and Second Life has led to meetings and events occurring in places which are not necessarily in one specific, fixed location. To illustrate this further, look at the think point below.

THINK POINT

Online communication technology (e.g. Skype) and virtual worlds (e.g. Second Life) allows events, meetings and conferences to take place without people being physically in the same place. Watch the following clip and answer the questions below: http://www.youtube.com/watch?v=m8F66mZdsHw&feature=related

To what extent do you think online meetings can replace meetings in real life? What might some of the advantages and disadvantages be of holding conferences in virtual worlds or through online communication technology?

To further explore the importance of place in the event context we can look at issues of landscape, sense of place, belonging and place identity.

Landscape

Different academic disciplines approach the notion of landscape from different viewpoints. The early understanding of landscape focused on the appearance of an area – the visual elements of the location – and was often associated with the countryside (Wylie 2009). Geography, where discussion of landscape is most prominent, has moved towards an awareness of the socio-cultural and political processes which continuously form landscapes.

Events often re-design and re-create the landscape of a place in a certain way, which can result in people seeing a place differently from their everyday perception of it. In Franconia, a wine region in southern Germany, many villages celebrate a weekend-long wine festival annually. For many of these festivals, local village and town centres are closed off and used as event sites. Thus, the everyday landscapes of a marketplace or a key road through the village are changed with tables, benches, stages and stalls. Another example of a change in landscape for event purposes can be seen in Figure 6.1, which shows a temporary, inflatable event venue used as part of Barcelona's fashion week 2011 and situated at Barcelona's water front.

Hirsch and O'Hanlon (1995) argue that it is due to cultural processes that an understanding of landscape is closely linked to issues of place and space, inside and outside, image and representation. In other words, our understanding of a place can

FIGURE 6.1 Temporary event venue, Barcelona
Source: © Teresa Leopold.

be influenced through a change in landscape, for example, through the introduction of a temporary event venue as shown in Figure 6.1, and thus, even for a potentially short period of time, this familiar place might develop into a festival place; our inside understanding of this place is therefore influenced by a change in landscape and we might see it from an outside, unfamiliar and external perspective. Of course, here we can make a link to Tuan's (1977) argument in that experience with the unfamiliar, such as a temporary festival landscape, changes it into a familiar place; for example, if you would attend the wine festival annually and little changes regarding how it is designed, you would be familiar with the festival landscape.

Next we want to turn our attention to the idea of sense of place; this will be followed by a discussion on the feeling of belonging and place identity.

Sense of place

The notion of a sense of place has been approached from different social science disciplines and fields of study, for example, social anthropology (Low and Lawrence-Zúñiga 2003), geography (Massey and Jess 1995) and cultural studies (Roberts 2012). This provides us with a complex collection of elements, which contribute to the development of a sense of place: on the one hand, sense of place is developed through geographic structures and characteristics of a place, the environmental setting and the knowledge of and interest in the local environment. On the other hand, it can be considered a social phenomenon through people's perceptions of, attachment to, experiences of and identification with places. For example, in his discussion of sheep farming in hill farms of the Scottish Borders, John Gray describes how shepherds name the features of the hills and cuts in which their sheep graze. 'As a referential practice, going around the hill also includes acts of naming places' (2003: 236). He goes on to argue that the naming of places by shepherds 'tames' the natural environment of the hills, and in so doing transforms them 'into places where they feel at home' (2003: 237): the process of naming gives a sense of place. This and the other approaches outlined above contribute to a sense of place, so that it is largely created through representations of and identifications with a place and through social interaction and practices by people.

THINK POINT

Think about the city where you are studying. How would you describe its sense of place? Consider various elements (physical and social), which might contribute to your understanding of its sense of place.

We can draw some clear links to the events context as it is exactly this feeling of a sense of place which is often celebrated through festivals and other regional events: 'The emotional attachment to a natural landscape and the built environment, climatic changes, and shared memories of communal heritage allow individuals to come together for formal or spontaneous interactions like festivals and community cultural events' (Derrett 2003: 50). Such happenings then provide opportunities for people to share culture through the event and create further place experiences, which in turn influences their sense of place and feeling of belonging and place identity. Before turning to the latter issues, the next case study demonstrates how different song festivals in Estonia present different feelings of sense of place and belonging.

CASE STUDY: ESTONIAN SONG FESTIVALS

Kuutma (1998) discusses three different song festivals in Estonia, which are held on a regular basis. Each festival, although representing an individual sense of place, celebrates different ethnic identities.

The Estonian national song festival *laulupidu* is a culturally constructed event which originated from culturally active intellectual Estonians adopting

Baltic German communal singing initiatives and song festivals. 'The inherited and the borrowed cultural elements resulted in the creation of a new version of the national culture module' (Dégh 1978: 43, cited in Kuutma 1998: 2). It is celebrated every five years with the 25th National Song Festival taking place in 2009. The key aim is to celebrate Estonian identity and includes national, regional and local song and dance festivals. Rural choirs that take part in the event often wear traditional nineteenth-century peasant costumes, while the festival itself is largely seen as a spectator experience.

The Setu song festival *leelopäev* is a small community event, which was initiated in the 1970s and takes place every three years. The festival is seen as a traditional community festival as it is organised by locals, the songs all represent the Setu tradition and dialect, people wear traditional costumes and traditional food is prepared. Thus, this festival celebrates a sense of place for the Setus, an ethnic group of Finno-Ugric origin who live in the south-eastern region of Estonia. Many former locals return to the area to join in the event.

The Slavic song and dance festival *Slavyanskiyvenok* was reintroduced in 1991 by the Slavic community after Estonia restored its independence. It largely derived from former Soviet citizens searching for their roots, their sense of belonging and a re-evaluation of Estonia as their home. Thus, this festival was developed to provide Russian, Ukrainian and Byelorussian communities in Estonia with a sense of place. Each ethnic group displays distinct colours, wears traditional customs and uses their native languages.

(*Source*: Kuutma 1998)

Belonging and place identity

The notion of belonging can be understood from different perspectives as people have different feelings of belonging to places and objects, which are underlined by different values (Yuval-Davis 2006). Thus, our feeling of belonging is not restricted to one place or one group of people but rather belonging is a dynamic process which can change with our life experiences and changes in values.

THINK POINT

To what locations, objects and groups do you feel a sense of belonging or attachment? Think about places where you have lived and groups and communities that you have joined. List as many as you can think of.

From the list that you developed, it should become apparent that the notion of belonging is very closely linked to the idea of identity, which we have explored in past chapters. Here it is important to note that different sociologists (such as Tönnies and Durkheim) have developed ways to explain changing forms of belonging due to a feeling of displacement, some of which have been briefly introduced in chapter 2 in the section on modernity.

Thus our identity (whether this be our gender, ethnicity, education, etc.) influences who and what we might belong to. These feelings of belonging influence our behaviour and actions or inactions but are not necessarily place specific. This is illustrated in Kirkup's (2012) study of the Olympics. She notes that people's social identity, social interaction and group affiliation provide them with a sense of belonging and thus motivate them to become Olympic tourists. Thus, belonging can be about the desire to belong to a group, as argued by Probyn (1996, cited in Yuval-Davis 2006: 202) 'Individuals and groups are caught within wanting to belong, wanting to become, a process that is fuelled by yearning rather than [the] positing of identity as a stable state', which, in turn, is one reason why people become involved in events.

Many studies have focused on the positive impacts that events can have upon communities' sense of belonging, such as Getz and Cheyne (2002) who argue that engagement and involvement in communal social and cultural processes, as well as the feeling of belonging and sharing, are some key motivational reasons for people to become involved in special events. This is illustrated in the case study 'Ritual revitalisation and the construction of places in Catalonia'.

CASE STUDY: RITUAL REVITALISATION AND THE CONSTRUCTION OF PLACES IN CATALONIA, SPAIN

Guiu (2008) studied 50 festivals in the Terres de l'Ebre region of south Catalonia, Spain. The region was marginalised for some time, not fitting well into the Autonomous Community of Catalonia, but has finally emerged as a 'traditional' and 'innovating' Catalan region. The area has capitalised on the revitalisation of 'old' festivals as well as the invention of 'new traditional festivals'. These new activities contribute to the making and uniting of regional identity.

The old and new festivals are different in terms of the discourses surrounding them. A village population might be brought together in a festival to celebrate a local saint and tends to be a celebration for 'insiders'. However, other festivals are engaged with by both locals and outsiders, with organisers putting together various scripts – brochures, stands, reports – which allow participants to both read about and understand the festival. The number of related publications has grown – guides, calendars, etc. – which leads to 'festive celebrations appear[ing] as mediums for developing images and representations of places' (Guiu 2008: 95).

Festivals are subject to processes of institutionalisation – they are 'officially' organised and subject to various cultural labels from an international (e.g. UNESCO) to a national and local level. Thus for a festival to be classified as traditionally Catalan it must satisfy certain criteria, including having its 'own cultural values and characteristics of the place where the festival is held' (Guiu 2008: 96), and will be awarded this recognition by the department of the *Generalitat*. The locations of festivals that have institutional recognition and are most strongly linked to Catalan identity show spatial groupings: 'they are principally concentrated around Barcelona and in the North; there are none in the Terres de l'Ebre Region' (Guiu 2008: 97). However, some are recognised for their importance for local interest by local councils.

Guiu identifies several kinds of festivals and notes that some contribute to both a sense of place and ideas of community. Some activities are particularly concerned with the promotion of a locality and are often organised by a specialist company or a local authority. A festival template is devised which can be 'localised', that is, given distinctive local characteristics that mark it as different from the same festival celebrated elsewhere. These are referred to by Guiu as 'adaptable festive kits'.

An example is the Móra Morisca festival in Móra d'Èbre, which was created in 1997 by local commission. The rationale behind the establishment of the festival was explained by one town counsellor: 'we wanted a festival related to the village, because we don't have anything special here, anything historical, typical, anything that identifies us' (Guiu 2008: 103). Much of the festival is organised by a professional events company, nevertheless local people decorate their houses and balconies, create costumes and sell items of food. In addition local 'traditional' craftsmen are invited to display their skills. The festival creates a sense of unity with participants reporting that the meaning of the festival is based on multiculturalism 'three cultures and only one world' (Guiu 2008:104). What these words refer to is the historical separation of Jewish, Christian and Muslim into three sectors symbolised in the festival by three doors, but in the celebrations these old division are overcome.

Other festivals are specifically about cohesion: 'Their prime purpose is to attract the population, to structure relationships and sociability' (Guiu 2008: 108). One example is the peasant festival in La Fatarella. Since 1994 the Farmers Union has been organising festivals that showcase rural life – demonstrations of farming practices, handicrafts, conferences about agriculture – which serve to illustrate rural values. The festivals are a response to concerns about the problems of developing rural zones and serve to show the vibrancy of the area. Attendees are not only farmers but also other elements of the population with an interest in the area, including bankers, academics and relatives of farmers. As such rural people are brought together in 'events to structure the agricultural sector, to reinforce sociability and to allow narratives on the inhabitants' (Guiu 2008: 110).

(*Source*: Guiu 2008)

However, we need to recognise that while certain events stimulate people to become involved due to reasons of belonging and identity, it is exactly these reasons why other people may actively exclude themselves or may be excluded from such a happening:

> The festival is, in fact, a paradoxical thing; festival events function as a form of social integration and cohesion, while simultaneously they are sites of subversion, protest or exclusion and alienation. It is precisely this paradoxical nature that creates the festival's socio-spatial and political significance for notions of community and belonging.
>
> (Duffy and Waitt 2011: 55)

Another point to note within the context of belonging and place identity is the wider meaning that events can have upon communities. Thus: 'Festivals help sustain narratives of belonging through bringing people together to share participating in various activities, but are also an exercise in remembering the past' (Duffy and Waitt 2011: 44). What elements of a history are remembered is often linked to people's willingness to remember or forget parts of the past (Cole 2003). Thus, events – particularly commemoration events – might remember a certain past while disregarding another as was noted during Bristol's International Festival of the Sea in 1996. While the aim of the event was to celebrate the city's naval maritime history, Bristol's role in the slave trade and imperialism was ignored (Atkinson and Laurier 1998). The importance of place, particularly for commemoration events, needs to be stressed here, however. Generally speaking, places of commemoration should enable people to understand the relationship of past, present and future (Hornstein 2003), should aid the development of place meaning and provide people with a clear sense of belonging to this place. This is further illustrated in the case study on the tsunami anniversary celebrations.

CASE STUDY: TSUNAMI ANNIVERSARY CELEBRATIONS

The tsunami of 26 December 2004 caused widespread death and destruction along coastal areas of many nations around the Indian Ocean. Lack of warning and practicable disaster management plans in any of the affected nations, coupled with the magnitude of the disaster, resulted in about 281,900 victims and made it one of the most destructive disasters recorded. Six Andaman provinces in the south of Thailand were affected by the tsunami disaster: Phuket, Trang, Phang Nga, Krabi, Ranong and Satun. The islands of Koh Phi Phi, near Phuket, are one of the most popular beach destinations in Thailand.

The Indian Ocean tsunami hit Koh Phi Phi Don on the morning of 26 December at 10.15 a.m. The terrain and built infrastructure of Koh Phi Phi made it highly vulnerable to the tsunami impact. Two waves hit the islands within five minutes of each other, one arriving at Ao Ton Sai and the other at the opposite beach Ao Loh Dalum. The sea on the beaches receded and then approached again with a massive force, colliding in the middle of the island and causing enormous destruction to human life and physical constructions. Following the tsunami, the streets on Koh Phi Phi Don were filled with rubble and waste, and many hotels, other accommodation, shops and paths were partly or totally destroyed. Of the 721 people who died in Krabi province, most died on Phi Phi Don.

Two commemoration celebrations were held on Koh Phi Phi during the first year: the Return to Paradise Carnival, marking the six-month anniversary of the tsunami and the One Year in Memory of Tsunami anniversary, which was celebrated throughout all affected Thai regions. The meanings and messages sent through the two events were slightly different; however the importance of place was apparent in both.

The Return to Paradise Carnival was organised by Thai and international volunteers to commemorate the disaster, 'promote the island being open for business' (Arnold 2006) and celebrate Koh Phi Phi's recovery six months after the tsunami disaster. It was largely organised by the organisation Help International Phi Phi (Hi Phi Phi) with support from the community. The carnival, 'whilst primarily an opportunity for the island to come together to celebrate, also worked as a great money-raiser' (Hi Phi Phi 2005d). The main celebrations took place in the most damaged area of the island, where hundreds of bungalows were located before the tsunami. This area 'was transformed into a party setting by myriad festive banners and decorations, along with the presence of many restaurants, bars and clothing stalls from around the island providing for the carnival guests' (Hi Phi Phi 2005).

Different sport tournaments, sandcastle competitions, snorkel treasure hunts, music performance and raffles were organised throughout the day; the celebrations finished with a fire dance show at midnight. Arnold (2006) describes the atmosphere as relaxed and joyous: 'A Thai reggae band played on the beach behind us while hundreds of young volunteers from every nationality danced in the sand.'

The One Year in Memory of Tsunami anniversary celebrations were organised by the Thai government with celebrations along the Andaman Coast from 25 December to 27 December 2005. The Royal Thai government utilised this event to achieve three objectives. One key aim was the commemoration of the disaster event as well as the victims of the tsunami (Phuket Press Center 2005a). It was further hoped that this renewed attention would provide a 'more thorough and accurate account of the rehabilitation work undertaken over the past year [and] will strengthen confidence and accentuate the positive aspects of tourism in the six affected provinces' (Phuket Press Center 2005a: 1).

The ceremony comprised four main sections: at 10.00, tsunami memorial services were held at seven venues, one of which was on Koh Phi Phi; at 16.20 the Tsunami Memorial Foundation stone-laying ceremony was organised in Khao Lak; at 18.20 the interfaith memorial services were held, also in Khao Lak; and at 20.30 a dinner reception was hosted by the Royal Thai government for about 500 VIPs. A total of 6,348 participants attended the memorial celebrations (Phuket Press Center 2005b). Dress codes were provided for the events, ranging from business attire to polite and light-coloured clothing.

These different anniversary celebrations show that the very nature of anniversaries is subject to the decision of whether and how memories of a disaster should be conserved, interpreted and reconstructed. The two anniversaries celebrated on Koh Phi Phi differed in their presented and intentional meaning; a key element of both events, however, was that they were celebrated on the islands of Koh Phi Phi where the actual disaster took place.

Reflecting on our discussion of the importance of belonging, it becomes clear that many festivals are developed through different narratives and stories which are presented as part of a place's history, individuals' attachment to a place and thus people's feeling of belonging. Thus, 'festivals can act as mirrors, reflecting a particular collective identity of a place through their program of events and activities' (Gibson *et al.* 2011: 12), so that places are presented in a certain way, as in history.

The presentation or representation of places can be explored in more detail by considering the approach of sociologist and philosopher Henri Lefebvre (1991) to the production of space, which is the subject of the next section.

The production of space

Lefebvre (1991) argues that space is not pre-given but comes about or is 'produced' through the dynamic interplay of three elements. What this approach allows us to do is to understand interaction between people – the social actors – in space and the ways in which space is represented. Thus in his analysis Lefebvre moves away from the idea that space is *a priori*, a container of action, to the idea that it is produced through the convergence of three different factors which give insights into the nature of social relationships.

The study of space offers an answer according to which the social relations of production have a social existence *to the extent that they have a spatial existence*; they project themselves into a space, becoming inscribed there, and in the process producing the space itself.

(Lefebvre 1991: 129, *emphasis in original*).

The three aspects of space that Lefebvre outlines are:

1 spatial practices
2 representation of space
3 representational space (sometimes translated as 'spaces of representation').

The first, *spatial practices*, refers to the 'facts' of space; that is, its physical or natural form. It is linked to the production and reproduction of specific places and spatial ensembles. As such an area may be developed for a particular activity or purpose.

The Shoton (yoghurt) festival in Tibet is celebrated with the unfurling of a giant Tibetan Buddhist Thangka (as can be seen on the front cover of the paperback version of this book). The festival marks the end of a period of seclusion and quiet contemplation for Buddhist monks. The revelation of the Thangka takes place on the side of a mountain – Mount Gambo – near to the Drepung Monastery. This monastery is considered to be the most important monastery for a particular school of Tibetan Buddhism. The site chosen for the unveiling of the Thangka relates to this but its positioning on the side of the mountain also connects to the rising sun. That is, as the sun rises the first rays of light will fall onto the Thangka (Xiao 2011). While we can see that this has religious significance we can also understand that the site is chosen specifically because its physical attributes allow the Thangka to face the rising sun and catch the first rays. It is the facts of the physical location and features of the mountain that inform the spatial practice of Mount Gambo as the chosen site to reveal the Thangka.

The second part of Lefebvre's formulation, *representations of space*, refers to formal abstractions. It is mental or conceived space. This is the space of the professionals or experts, for example: event organisers, planners, policy makers, architects, cartographers and designers. Here space is constructed and formalised around ideological discourses relating to how the professionals want a particular space to be represented. This produces various representations or media, such as maps, exhibition guides, brochures, plans of buildings, event venues, various forms of electronic media, advertising and marketing material. This aspect of space relates to how the professionals, who also hold power, want everybody else to see, understand and use the space and this in turn reproduces social relations.

THINK POINT

Look at the map for Glastonbury 2011 (Figure 6.2). Notice how the site of the festival is divided into different activities, for example, lounging and viewing area, healing field, camping. Make a list of all the different designated spaces.

GLASTONBURY FESTIVAL 2011

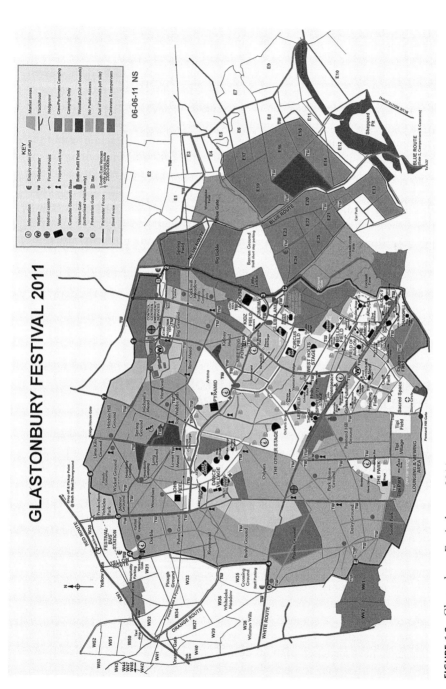

FIGURE 6.2 Glastonbury Festival map, 2011

Source: © Glastonbury Festival Ltd.

The map of Glastonbury provides a representation of space. However, the spatial organisation also reflects how the festival's spaces have evolved through lived experiences, which brings us to the third aspect of space that Lefebvre (1991) identifies, called *spaces of representation*. This element is concerned with the ways in which space is lived, the world of the senses and what people actually do in a given place. For Lefebvre it is the space in which resistance to the hegemony of *spatial practice* and *representations of space* can be acted upon. As such it can become a site of resistance. Looking back at the Glastonbury Festival map, if festival goers decided to pitch a tent in the healing field, then they would be resisting or reacting against the power of the festival organisers by trying to use the space differently from the use to which it has been assigned. It is through this lived experience of space that Lefebvre argues changes can be brought about. If everybody decided to set up camp in the healing field, then the purpose of this field as designated by the festival organisers would be overturned. A similar scenario is illustrated in Figure 6.3, which shows how a monument in Dublin is turned into a viewing platform during the St Patrick's Day Parade.

Spaces of representation links in with ideas of performance discussed in chapter 4, as it places an emphasis on what people do and how they interact with their surroundings. In chapter 4 we discussed how performing connects to taking part, to practice, and it is to this that *spaces of representation* relates. The case study about public nudity in Canada illustrates the point.

CASE STUDY: IS IT PERMISSIBLE FOR WOMEN TO BARE THEIR BREASTS IN ALL PUBLIC SPACES?

In Canada, as in many countries around the world, women are not allowed to go topless in public but men are. On hot days people may visit a park or beach to relax in the sun or sunbathe. Men are allowed to be bare-chested in all these spaces, women only on nudist beaches. The fact that women are not permitted to bare their breasts in the same way as men undermines the principles of equal opportunities and serves to reinforce ideas of women as sexualised beings and in turn reinforces gendered social relations. This unequal treatment led to women resisting the dominant legal codes restricting female nudity in public. In 1991, one woman decided to walk the streets of Guelph, Ontario Canada revealing her breasts. 'She stated that it was a deliberate political act intended to protest the censure of a woman who bares her breasts, when men who do the same are ignored' (Morton 2011: 611).

Acts of resistance regarding how women may bare their bodies in public appear to have increased both inside and outside Canada, with the attached rhetoric (or language) of supporting equal rights for women. For example 'Go Topless' and the 'Top Free Equal Rights Association' (TERA) have both staged protest demonstrations.

(*Source*: http://gotopless.org; http://www.tera.ca)

FIGURE 6.3 Different usage of space, Dublin, 2010

Source: © Teresa Leopold.

As noted, *representations of space* are seen to be very powerful because they are understood to influence the way that people behave and sometimes, as in the case of women baring their breasts or not in Canada, are inscribed in law. One of the key providers of representations is electronic media. We consider the role of the media in developing and shaping events in the next section.

Role of media

Media can be separated into two types: print media (for example books, magazines, newspapers, comics) and non-print or electronic media (for example television – terrestrial and satellite, world wide web, DVDs, cinema and radio). We can also draw distinctions between private and public domains, for example, personal holiday photos versus holiday brochures or destination websites. With the advent of the internet and other advances in technology the daily lives of many people, particularly in the western world, are infused with the media.

To understand the role of media within the event context we first need to consider what it means. The word 'media' relates to both the practice of broadcasting and the dissemination of information by other means. Thus, media are 'in the middle' between an audience and the event(s) reported. The reporters, newscasters and commentators are mediating what has happened, relaying the story to the viewer (see Figure 6.4).

We can see, then, that whoever is making the report, editing the programme and so on will be making a *representation of space* (Lefebvre 1991) insofar as they produce an abstract representation of what that space is, by implication, used for, and, as discussed in the preceding section, helping to inform our ideas of what a place and/or situation is like. The case study 'Bad news from Israel' examines this idea in more detail.

FIGURE 6.4 Media representatives during the Olympic Torch Relay, 2012

Source: © Les Roberts.

CASE STUDY: BAD NEWS FROM ISRAEL

In a study of news broadcasts about the Palestinian–Israeli conflict and their impacts on audiences, Philo and Berry (2004) interviewed journalists and broadcasters and analysed TV news coverage of Israel between September 2000 and April 2002. They also investigated audience responses through the use of questionnaires and focus groups.

The analysis of the news reporting showed that it was dominated by the Israeli perspective. Palestinians were seen as the source of trouble and Israel as only responding to Palestinian aggression or retaliating. The news demonstrated more coverage of Israeli casualties than Palestinian, although in reality there were more Palestinian casualties. There was also a different type of language used to discuss the casualties on both sides, with the Israeli deaths being described as 'mass murder'.

Philo and Barry also found that the news reports lacked the historical context of the conflict and that constraints in the production process of news reports – time, concerns for audience ratings – favoured images of violence, fighting and destruction instead of explanations. Rather than an explanation of the events, there was a focus on bombings that fuelled American and Israeli perspectives about the so-called 'War on Terror'.

The findings from the research with the audience participants demonstrated that people did not understand key elements of the conflict, saw it as being initiated by the Palestinians and the Israelis as merely responding. The audience in effect reproduced the themes of the news.

(*Source*: Philo and Berry 2004)

The Palestinian–Israeli situation is highly politicised and violent, but not all cases of political use of the media are associated with such obvious forms of conflict. Media and various forms of events have had a long and intertwined relationship. Roche (2000: 160) comments on the importance of media for World Exhibitions (Expos) in terms of promoting 'media-related technologies'. For example, telephones were on show for the first time to mass audiences as part of the Philadelphia Expo of 1876. In addition, the media have been used to generate publicity. For example, technological developments in photography around the late 1800s meant greater media exposure of Expos via newspapers and the development of picture postcards as tourist souvenirs. Clearly there have been even greater advances in technology since this time and Roche (2000: 162) points to the importance of radio as a means to 'enable a mass nationwide listening audience to imagine that they are present at a dramatic and important "live" event'. This argument can be mirrored when thinking about TV broadcasts and live feeds on the world wide web. In particular, the spread of social media has resulted in an increasing proliferation of non-professional mediators of realities (for example, the use of Facebook and Twitter during the Arab Spring).

There has been a growth of the relationship between media and events with increasing amounts of live coverage of sporting fixtures (Olympics, the football World Cup) and national events (royal weddings, swearing-in of presidents), which can have overtly political connotations, such as the radio broadcasting of the 1936 Berlin Olympics (Roche 2000).

THINK POINT

Reflect on some of the events that you observed through different forms of media. What kind of events were they? Why did you choose to take part in the event by watching it, listening to it or reading about it?

The discussion of the relationship between events and the media has been framed by a dramatological perspective and draws on theories of ritual (some of which are outlined in chapter 3) developed after van Gennep (1960) by Victor Turner (Roche 2000). That is, the broadcasting of the events is usually 'marked by a clear beginning and ending that interrupts normal social routines, they feature heroic personalities, they are highly dramatic or richly symbolic, and they are accompanied by social norms which relate to their special character' (Roche 2000: 163). Drawing on the work of Dayan and Katz (1987, 1988, 1992), Roche argues it is possible to identify 'media-events', which he says can be recognised by the fact 'that people in many nations feel obliged to watch and feel privileged to be able to witness the event' (Roche 2000: 164). These activities are seen to be different, requiring different treatment from the everyday broadcasting of news or entertainment, and are often associated with ideas of 'making history'. Events that fall into this category include the Moon landings, the funeral of Diana, Princess of Wales and political occasions, for example the release of Nelson Mandela from prison in South Africa in 1990.

THINK POINT

The French philosopher Jean Baudrillard (1995) argued that the Gulf War of 1992 did not actually happen but was a carefully crafted media event. Think about what he could mean by this argument.

The modern Olympic Games can be understood as 'a multi-genre event displaying spectacle, ritual and festival dimensions as well as the game dimension' (Roche 2000:165). This is a complex mix of genres, of which the most important element is the spectacle; it has been argued that the balance between them has been altered by global TV broadcasting (MacAloon 1981, 1984, 1989, 1992 in Roche 2000: 165). An issue that needs to be considered when thinking about such so-called 'media-events' is that the broadcast will be subject to editing and, as such, a particular discourse will be developed around the event. 'Olympic TV addresses itself to presenting ... a unitary event, prioritising some (dominant, official) perspectives and narratives over others' (Roche 2000: 166). This, in turn, changes the nature of participation in the event as the viewing audience cannot engage in the same way as if they were actually there but rather are subject 'to a logic of programming, sequential focus and pace' (Roche 2000: 166).

It is possible to identify the modern Olympic movement and associated TV coverage as having characteristics of modernity (see chapter 2) if we follow some of the arguments developed by MacAloon, namely, that the Olympics try to convey meta-narratives of, for example, peaceful nationalism and rationality (Roche 2000). However, Michael Real (1989, 1995, 1996a, 1996b, 1996c, 1996d, 1998) argues that Olympic TV coverage is more closely related to ideas of postmodernism (see chapter 2) due to the commercialisation of the event and the 'information overload' presented through the numerous images and messages being broadcast. Not only that, but the overarching messages identified as part of the modernist paradigm can only partially be portrayed (Roche 2000).

The purpose of this section is to draw attention to the role of media in events. It is a complex area of discussion and we have only outlined a few approaches not just to illustrate the links between media and events but also to highlight how some of the social science theories discussed earlier (for example modernity and postmodernity in chapter 2 and ritual in chapter 3) find their way into different areas of debate in literature related to events. As technology continues to develop we would expect to see even more discussion about the relationship between media and the many varied forms of events that are transmitted to us.

Summary

In this chapter we explored:

- the connection between space and place and representation;
- the changing nature of landscape in relation to events;
- the role of place in creating a sense of belonging;
- how space can be produced, lived and challenged;
- the role of media in how places and people are represented in connection to events.

Suggested reading

Gibson, C. and Connell, J. (eds) (2011) *Festival Places: Revitalising Rural Australia*. Bristol: Channel View.

Lefebvre, H. (1991) *The Production of Space*. Oxford: Blackwell.

Roche, M. (2000) *Mega Events and Modernity: Olympics and Expos and the Growth of Global Culture*. London: Routledge.

Sardar, Z. and Van Loon, B. (2000) *Introducing Media Studies*. Cambridge: Icon Books.

Shields, R. (1999) *Lefebvre, Love and Struggle: Spatial Dialectics*. London: Routledge.

Useful websites

Second Life: http://secondlife.com

Virtual Festivals: http://www.virtualfestivals.com

Estonian Song and Dance Festival: http://estonia.eu/about-estonia/culture-a-science/song-and-dance-festivals.html

Glastonbury Festival: http://www.glastonburyfestivals.co.uk

Koh Phi Phi – Return to Paradise Carnival: www.hiphiphi.com/24june/Return-to-Paradise.doc

7

HABITUS, THE BODY AND GENDER

In this chapter we wish to explore three key areas that contribute to our understanding of the practices and experiences of events. Each one of these themes could be discussed as a separate entity, but we have chosen to discuss them in one chapter because they have the potential to interweave with each other to contribute to the formation of the praxis of these things we label events. We will begin with the concept of *habitus* as it provides an understanding of a range of different ideas explored and touched upon in earlier chapters. For example, consumption, discussed in detail in chapter 5, is closely linked to *habitus* in that what people consume creates a sense of who they are. Similarly, remembering our discussion of the changes in social status over the last few centuries, in chapter 2, we can see that during modern times *habitus* allows for an understanding of a more fluid and mobile state, as it allows for change, from alterations of one's preferences to changes of social class. At the same time, *habitus* is also useful to highlight some of the issues that still need to be discussed when exploring events in a social science context, namely the senses, embodiment, the symbolic body and the role of gender. This chapter, then, will discuss the following:

- the concept of habitus
- the importance of embodiment and the senses
- the symbolic body
- issues of gendered perspectives.

Habitus

In chapter 2 we identified the notions of structure and agency and the conflict that can arise between the two. One way of understanding how they work together is through the concept of *habitus*. The way in which we are using the concept is derived first from the work of Marcel Mauss (1979) and its further development by Pierre Bourdieu (1977, 1979, 1990). The basic idea underpinning the concept is an attempt to understand how the external environment or structure is internalised and interpreted differently by different social actors. As such, *habitus* is 'a set of dispositions which incline agents to act and react in a certain way' (Thompson 1991: 12). Thus, it is argued that how we use our bodies and our responses (both emotional and physiologically) to the world in general are influenced by our social background and the values attributed to our tastes, and these in turn serve to legitimise our actions and dispositions. The social background includes class, gender, race, ethnicity and so on.

Our *habitus* is argued to be formed by our earliest social experiences and associated socialisation processes. We learn to like certain types of entertainment, which can influence the types of events we choose to be involved in. For example allegiance to a particular football team is likely to be derived from growing up alongside people who support the same team. We can make similar observations about television programmes, and interest in other forms of entertainment, for example cinema and theatre. This is not to say that individuals do not develop their own interests but rather that early influences can remain very powerful throughout life. As noted, part of our social background includes class and it is argued that the choices we exercise in relation to events can act as class markers if we draw a distinction between so-called 'high-art' events (operas or ballet performances, for example) as opposed to so-called 'popular cultural' events, such as bingo nights and pier-end entertainment shows.

The concept of *habitus* is linked by Bourdieu to the notion of 'field', which refers to the context or arena in which action takes place; so the high-arts present one field and popular culture another. The argument is based on the idea that knowledge of how to behave in a field of action, which Bourdieu calls 'cultural capital', comes from our socialisation in a particular *habitus*. Thus, one's *habitus* defines one's preferences and tastes. What we have to remember is that

> people are comfortable when there is a correspondence between habitus and field ... otherwise people feel ill at ease and seek to move – socially and spatially – so that their discomfort is relieved ... mobility is driven as people, with their relatively fixed habitus, both move between fields ... and move to places within fields where they feel more comfortable.
>
> (Savage *et al.* 2005: 9)

THINK POINT

Reflect on your tastes in humour, music and sport. Can you attribute these to your upbringing or how do you think they have been shaped?

You may have expressed tastes or preferences that you cannot relate to your early background. This is because, as we have observed, tastes can change and develop. *Habitus* can be adjusted and altered. For example, you can learn how to speak differently, like new and/or different foods and change your taste in entertainment. *Habitus*, then is not a static state of being but rather has potential for change and can be developed.

Within the context of events, one's *habitus* might influence, among others, what events we go to, why we go to certain events, our interest in certain events, our behaviour at events and even our willingness to become involved (through volunteering or donation) in charity events. For example, many motivational studies linked to tourism (such as McIntosh and Goeldner 1986; Cleaver *et al.* 2000), but also events (such as Crompton and McKay 1997; Bennett *et al.* 2007), have highlighted the role of status in one's reasoning about going on holiday or attending an event. For example, Chang and Yuan (2011) highlight the importance of socialisation including 'to be with people who enjoy the same things' as an important motivational factor for event attendance. It is not our intention to explore motivational studies in more detail here, but rather to reiterate that the idea that *habitus* can influence one's decision processes as to whether to attend an event or not.

CASE STUDY: ART OUTSIDE THE GALLERY

Three artists Martin Goodrich, Jim Ives and Barbara Wheeler-Early were all trained as fine artists and were keen to use their knowledge and skills outside of the conventional art gallery system and thus founded an organisation that eventually became known as Free Form Arts Trust. The artists were keen to engage working-class people and to create art with them as well as for them. Goodrich's explanation of the reasoning behind the project was to take art to 'the great [public] housing estates in England where art meant nothing' (Crehan 2011: 31). A studio was established for Goodrich and Ives in a temporary building on Jutland Road in the East End London district of Plaistow. The area surrounding the road was working-class and provided no real playgrounds for the local children who became intrigued by what was happening in the studio. The artists were trying to work on a project to be included in an Arts Council funded initiative and needed to find a way of dealing with the children's curiosity about what they were doing. Thus, they began to run workshops that allowed the children to create art works for themselves while the artists simultaneously worked on their exhibition piece. Although the purpose of the exhibition funded by the Arts Council was to showcase new forms of displaying and engaging with art, Goodrich and Ives felt that it was still closely linked to 'the gallery system' and they began to realise that they wanted to be more inclusive of the children they had been working with. They were joined by Wheeler-Early and decided to stage a community-based exhibition called the 'Free Form Fun Event' over a weekend 'where the "participating" audience was not a typical art event audience' (Crehan 2011: 47).

(*Source*: Crehan 2011)

What this case study demonstrates is that until the arrival of the artists in the area the children were not being socialised into a world which included art practices. We could therefore argue that their *habitus* was being shaped into one that would perhaps not go on to engage with art. However, with Free Form the children's existing knowledge of and engagement in the world had the potential to change through the daily workshop events put on by the artists and, further, they had the opportunity to take part in and view an exhibition, which may previously have been unavailable to them.

The concept of *habitus* is closely linked to ideas of embodiment, which refers to the ways in which we use our bodies in an unconscious way to do things. Therefore, the way the body moves and the involvement of the senses (sight, touch, hearing, taste and smell) all become important areas of consideration. In western society the far senses of sight and hearing have tended to be privileged – with sight being the most important – over the near senses of touch, taste and smell (Falk 1994). In the next section we will consider aspects of sensory experiences and their importance to events. We will begin with the role of sight and the significance of the gaze, which will also serve as a useful backdrop against which to highlight the importance of other senses.

The senses

The idea of the gaze became prominent through the work of Michel Foucault (1976, 1977), who argues that power could be exercised in the form of surveillance and looking. Based on Bentham's (1748–1832) Panopticon (this is a type of building – often a prison – designed so that the guards can easily see the inmates of the gaol without them knowing when they are being observed. The idea is that in being aware of the possibility of being watched a form of 'self-policing' is encouraged, in that behaviour will be modified to ensure that one is not seen to break institutional rules.) Foucault identifies that people's behaviour can be controlled simply by their being watched. This idea was developed further by John Urry (1990, 2002) in relation to tourism, whereby he argues that 'the gaze' is a central organising feature of tourism activity, as the basis of tourism activity is going to look at sites of difference. During this, people and places at tourist destinations are consumed by tourists in the act of looking. This can also be applied to the event context, as can

FIGURE 7.1 Gazing and capturing event experiences

Source: © Les Roberts.

be seen in Figure 7.1, which shows the consumption of an event through the act of seeing and taking photographs.

Urry (1990, 2002) comments that our gaze is:

- socially organised and systemised;
- a learned ability; and that
- the pure and innocent eye is a myth (that is we look at things with pre-understanding of what it is we are looking at).

These ideas are developed further in a later edition of Urry's book: 'people gaze upon the world through a particular filter of ideas, skills, desires and expectations, framed by social class, gender, nationality, age and education' (Urry and Larsen 2011: 2). As such, there are different ways of interpreting what we see and this applies as much to events as to tourism practices. For example the Festival of Saint Sara in the south of France in the month of May attracts a large number of visitors to observe 'an event they see as ancient, primitive, primeval, traditional, and, above all, authentic' (Stanley 2007: 243). However, as Urry and Larsen (2011) mention we need to remember that our gaze is socio-culturally framed and, as such, we also need to remember that there are different ways of 'seeing'. This brings us back to our discussion on *habitus*, in that our social background and values influence our expectations and perceptions of an event experience, and ultimately how we 'see' an event. Similarly, think back to our discussion on the different roles of performers during an event (in chapter 4); depending on whether you are, for example, an exhibitor, a stage performer or an audience member, you would 'gaze upon' and interpret an event differently.

THINK POINT

Give an interpretation of what is happening in the picture and compare your answer to someone else's.

FIGURE 7.2   Interpretation of an event

Source: © Martha Noyes.

At the same time that we go to events to watch, as mentioned in chapter 4, the participants are the objects of surveillance not only by each other but also by systems of surveillance such as CCTV cameras, security and police. For example, Andrews and Roberts (2012) note that an impromptu beach party on Margate beach was being monitored by a mobile police CCTV van. The purpose of this is not simply to monitor what is happening but because the knowledge that they are being watched affects the behaviour of the party goers. Similarly, the Olympic Torch Relay in the United Kingdom in 2012 was accompanied by a heavy police presence and cameras. In Chester (a city in the north-west of England) the route of the relay

FIGURE 7.3 CCTV camera sign

Source: © Hazel Andrews.

was marked on some roads by street decorations in the form of the torch. While noting the symbolic value of these artefacts we are also reminded that we are not only looking but are also being looked at (see Figure 7.3).

THINK POINT

Watch the following clip about the Goth Festival in Whitby online: http://www.youtube.com/watch?v=QZXSMLoG0fw

What is discussed about gazing? While watching the clip, also consider yourself as actively gazing at the event. What are some of the elements that you are gazing upon? How do you feel about gazing at the Goth culture?

CASE STUDY: WHITBY GOTH FESTIVAL

Whitby, a seaside resort in the north-east of England, has been host to the Whitby Goth Festival since 1994. Bram Stoker, the author of *Dracula*, was inspired by the setting of the village and started writing his book in 1890. The town's scenery, with the ruins of St Hilda's Abbey, St Mary's church and its graveyard on the East Cliff, appear in parts of Stoker's story:

> But, strangest of all, the very instant the shore was touched, an immense dog [Dracula] sprang up on deck from below . . . and running forward, jumped from the bow on to the sand. Making straight for the steep cliff, where the churchyard hangs over the laneway to the East Pier . . . it disappeared in the darkness.

In the story, Dracula slept in a grave in the churchyard during his time in Whitby. It is largely this association with Dracula, which inspired the first meeting of about 200 Goths in 1994, held at a local pub, The Elsinore. Since then, Whitby has played host to the Whitby Goth Festival twice a year (apart from 2011, when the festival took place over four weekends) and has attracted increasing numbers of people who take part in the 'undead carnival'.

The Goth culture emerged from punk rock in the late 1970s and reflects a balance between different types of contradictions: grotesque and beautiful; authentic self-expression and campness; cult following and mass appeal (Spooner 2006, cited in Goulding and Saren 2009). The Goth scene is thus varied, with a passion for the dark aesthetic, music preferences ranging from folk music to heavy metal and expressive punk to baroque music, and clothing which some associate with horror imagery. There are varied sub-cultures or sub-groups within the Goth culture such as cyber-Goths and Edwardian Goths. In its beginnings, the Goth culture was considered a youth culture but has developed into a much more diverse community so that age groups attending the festival can vary from young children who attend with their parents to teens and older people.

The Whitby Goth Festival has now developed into something larger than just a celebration of Goths, with many costume dressers promenading the small streets of Whitby, 'Goth spotters' who come to soak up the atmosphere and ambience of the town and gaze at Goths, and photographers who dominate the street by frequently asking people to pose for them or who just take pictures. This exposure, gazing and consuming, has increased enormously during recent years, to an extent where it has now led to actions being taken by the Goth community and Whitby. Thus, in April 2012 a press release was published on the Whitby Goth Festival website (2012):

> The organisers of the Whitby Goth Weekend have produced thousands of information cards for distribution at its 2012 events following a large influx of photographers to the North Yorkshire seaside town which is seemingly now having a detrimental effect on both the event and the enjoyment of its visitors. The cards serve as a polite request for respect from photographers and also serve as a warning to those considered to be acting in an inappropriate manner. Promoter Jo Hampshire said 'We're very honoured that so many people wish to capture our special weekend but we are appealing for respect to those who may not wish to have their picture taken and that photographers have the courtesy to ask before taking photographs.'

It is largely this influx in photographers, which has led to a ban of pictures being taken of people posing on or against gravestones at the St Mary's Hill churchyard. This was announced by the rector of the Church on St Mary's Hill shortly before the festival in October 2011 and initially caused an uproar among Goths, photographers and other visitors. However, as Jo Hampshire explains on the Goth Festival website (2012):

> While I personally don't have a problem with people posing on or near gravestones (and have myself in the past), as long as you are careful not to ruin them or be respectful if there is anyone actually visiting them and stay away – I think they are beautiful objects and make for wonderful photographs. There are of course people who disagree with that on religious or other grounds. Indeed I think doing provocative or scantily clad shots in graveyards are in poor taste, but similarly some would think simply being Goth in a graveyard is in poor taste – so it's all just a matter of perspective. However I still agree with the ban. Why? Because it was getting out of hand. Myself and anyone else who tried to walk up to the Abbey just to enjoy the view was besieged by photographers, some being quite polite and actually asking to take your picture (although after the 20th time even this politeness grates on you) with others just taking pictures without asking. Some, when they are turned down, act

shocked and a little nasty. Once when I was walking along the waterfront a lovely elder [sic] lady with a professional camera approached me and asked ever so nicely if she could take my picture, this time I agreed. Just then she beckoned to her male friend, and moments later I had the two of them shooting me and requesting that I pose like this, do this, look that way. I don't ever say yes anymore.

The *Whitby Gazette* (2011) writes:

> In some cases people have been photographed laid or even stood on tombstones, and after viewing examples of these the Whitby Goth Weekend contacted St Mary's Church offering full backing to their decision. A statement was released to this effect and this support still stands . . . Although the churchyard closed in 1861, it is hallowed ground and contains the tombstones of many local Whitby families who continue to this day to scatter the ashes of loved ones in the churchyard.

This influx of photographers has caused additional concerns as gazing and photography can quickly lead to the objectification of people, particularly women. Goulding and Saren (2009) researched gender expressions at the Goth Festival and argue that the Goth culture puts 'the "curves" back in the feminine' and allows both sexes to flaunt the female within so that the Goth culture allows for a blurring of gender boundaries and a privileging of the female. However, with the number of photographers increasing enormously in the last few years, objectifying the female has become an increasing concern for the organisers, as illustrated in the observations posted on the official Whitby Goth Festival website (2012):

> Back at the Abbey crowds of photographers, mostly men, gather round a young girl (in an outfit perfectly acceptable as goth [sic] attire – but you must understand what we deem normal make some men rub their legs with glee when they are able to encounter it). As EOS-Phil from canon-fodder-forums.com puts it, 'Where else can you photograph girls in their underwear without getting arrested? Unless you have a long lens.' And he isn't the only one who has this view. Technoblurb from pentaxuser.co.uk asks, 'Now is it the guys in drag your [sic] getting exited [sic] about or the very strange woman with the bull whip' and greynolds999 answers, 'Perhaps it's the opportunity of photographing cleavage and stockings without getting arrested!' and goes on to say, 'Actually, let's not bother with all the heavy camera gear this time. Turn up, oggle, breakfast, oggle, beer, oggle, home.' And it's hard to see how Technoblurb doesn't realize how things are getting out of hand when he says, 'Great eye contact David in the "That look" shot, although I am

embarrassed to admit that the first thing I spotted was the mucky lens mark in her cleavage." But greynolds999's comment in another thread is very telling of what an excuse their camera really is, saying it's not really possible to get away with 'asking girls to put whips in their teeth and show you their stockings if you don't have a camera.' They then post the picture greynolds999 was referring to and fatspider adds, 'And yes it was Gareth that asked her to put the whip between her teeth'. The comments under another posted image again objectifies yet another girl: gtis wrote: '[I] am surprised you looked at her face'. fatspideranswered 'Face? Oh she has a face.' And when [the] topic goes on to one of a more technical nature davidtrout [sic] urges 'enough talk of software, lets [sic] look at the girls.' But trying to raise the tone slightly, greynolds999 says 'This year we must take pictures of at least one man! . . .' Technoblurbreplies '. . . Flanked by two scantily dressed ladies' and Father Ted adds 'I took photos of a man. OK, only because he wouldn't move far enough out of shot when I was getting a photo of his wife!!' The predatory nature of these photographers is aptly described in this comment by gtis when all he could get was the photo of the back of a latex-clad subject, "[G]areth and me where waiting for her to come out of the shop, [I] think she knew we where [sic] waiting so [I] just took a few shots in between people walking in front of us.' While fatspider helpfully critiques the photo by saying, 'that skirt needs to be a foot shorter.'

As we have noted, there are other senses, besides sight to be considered as part of our experiences in the world.

THINK POINT

Note down the bodily sensations that you felt at an event that you have attended.

Some of the body sensations that you might have noted down could be feeling cold, sweating, getting wet, being sunburned, thirsty and or being hungry. All of these can be experienced as part of an event whether as a member of the audience or as a performer. For example, Mayes (2011: 164) says of Raventhorpe's Wildflower Show, Australia, that it 'celebrates subjective emotional and aesthetic pleasures and ways of knowing', noting that people report on the importance of smells and the ambience of the flowers drawing attention to the perfumes and the colours encountered.

If we put too much emphasis on the gaze it means that we miss other aspects of the experiential nature of events. Consider, for example, the importance of taste and smell at a food festival, and of touch when standing in the front rows of large-scale music concerts. Other aspects include emotions, people's feelings, bodily sensations and the ways in which the body is used. Duffy and Waitt (2011: 48) study emotion and the body in relation to rural festivals in Australia and note that 'Emotions, how they are absorbed by individuals and transferred between bodies … play a crucial part in the relationships created and built up between people, place and festivals.' This brings us on to ideas of embodiment.

Embodiment

What this term refers to is the centrality of our bodies in how we encounter the world and how we engage actions unconsciously. Marcel Mauss (1979) argued that we have particular ways of using our bodies which we learn and internalise and thus we practise certain actions without thinking about the actual movements involved. For example, in many forms of dance, when we dance we move our bodies in time to the music without thinking 'now I must move my leg here and my arm there'. Even in very formal dancing, the practitioners have embodied the moves they need to perform and do not necessarily consciously think about the next step. The use of the body through dance is illustrated in Figure 7.4, which shows the Sycamore

FIGURE 7.4 Movement of body as part of a dance performance

Source: © Martha Noyes.

Lawn Mower Brigade, USA, during the 4 July parade in 2012. The performers, mostly middle-aged white suburban men with little rhythm or dance skills, dance in formation with their lawn mowers.

Some social scientists – for example Michael Jackson (1989) and Alfred Gell (1996) – argue that human experience is grounded in the movement and way of being of the body, which is itself set within the framework of the material or social environment. Thus, an examination of body uses and experiences gives an indication of ideas about the world. According to Jackson, there is a psychophysical relationship with the world. He uses the example of falling over. We can literally physically fall over and we can also experience a fall mentally as in a fall from grace for example. As such, a fall can occur both in the mind and body. Jackson also argues that a disruption to the environment can lead to changes to bodily dispositions. In trying to understand an apparent role reversal between men and women during an initiation ceremony of the Kuranko people (based in West Africa), Jackson (1989: 129) argues that it is the change in *habitus* brought about by the enactment of the ceremony and initiation rites that gives rise to the change in actions by members of the community and thus 'lays people open to possibilities of behavior which they embody, but ordinarily are not inclined to express'. We can see this kind of disruption occurring in other kinds of events. For example, an event organised to raise money for the Samaritans used role reversal as the attraction. The chefs took on the role of the waiters and waiters were chefs for one evening. Customers were then asked to pay as much as they thought the dining experience was worth.

In thinking about how we use our bodies we also need to consider how it is adorned in terms of costumes and clothes that people wear. By putting on a costume people often turn into the character they are trying to portray and then use their body differently from when out of character (Figure 7.5).

Another example is the 'cosplay' culture. Cosplay stands for 'costume' and 'play' and refers to people who dress and re-enact their favourite *anime*, manga or video game character in cosplay communities through events and conventions. As Winge (2006: 65) explains: 'Cosplayers spend immeasurable monies and hours constructing or purchasing costumes, learning signature poses and dialogue, and performing at conventions and parties, as they transform themselves from "real world" identities into chosen (fictional) characters'. Other examples include different heritage events, for example re-enactments of medieval celebrations or the American civil war where people put on costumes and take on a specific character that they are portraying during the event. Knox and Hannam (2007: 269) discuss how Viking re-enactment performances focus on displaying masculinity through 'masculine displays of strength and skill', with re-enactment of roles ranging from warriors to craftsmen. This focus on displaying the 'authentic' roles of masculinity (e.g. warriors) and femininity (e.g. weavers) of the Viking past presents a re-enactment of conservative gender roles, which would not be tolerated in modern Norway. Thus, embodiment in the event context can present complex symbolic meanings, as further illustrated in the case study 'Woman, body, space – Rio Carnival and the politics of performance'.

FIGURE 7.5   German tourists dressed up for the St Patrick's Day celebrations in Dublin, 2010

Source: © Teresa Leopold.

CASE STUDY: WOMAN, BODY, SPACE – RIO CARNIVAL AND THE POLITICS OF PERFORMANCE

Lewis and Pile (1996) discuss how women's bodies and performance of women's bodies during the Rio Carnival present contradictory cultural meanings and values. This is particularly apparent in terms of public versus privatised space in that 'the woman who dances samba in the street is marked as different from the woman who remains at home' (Lewis and Pile 1996: 35). Women who thus move from a private into a public space risk being perceived as dirty and likely to disgrace themselves (Pollock 1988, cited in Lewis and Pile 1996: 35), particularly as the Brazilian public space is often considered as masculinised. At the same time, women who perform in public spaces are scrutinised through complex power relations (such as gender, race), which in turn strengthen such distinctive values.

In the context of the Rio Carnival, the bodies of 'paraders' are controlled through expectations of beauty and, since the early 1990s, nakedness has been increasingly common among performers (female, male and child). However it is largely the female body which is criticised so that 'women have become their bodies, they wear their bodies as a costume'. This focus on naked women's bodies strengthens the risk of 'being seen as "out of place" and in breaking the rule of feminine domesticity' (Lewis and Pile 1996: 34) and thus presenting conflicting values to the traditional values of feminine domesticity.

(*Source*: Lewis and Pile 1996)

As we can see from the examples and case study above, embodiment becomes a crucial element in many forms of celebrations, festivals, carnivals and other happenings through the use of costumes and people's performances and behaviour. Without undermining the importance of the senses and ideas of embodiment to our understanding of experiences and practices of events we need to consider that the body and how it is dressed can also have a symbolic role, which is the subject of the next section.

Symbolic bodies

At the basis of an understanding of the symbolic body is the idea put forward by social scientists that the body is socially and culturally constructed. As such, it is a means of expression. For example, a tattoo can symbolise membership of a gang, the make-up worn by punks and Goths can symbolise attachment to those groups. An event-related example of using one's body as a form of expression can be seen in Figure 7.6. What should be noted here is that the person in the picture has no Irish roots and that he had the tattoo done the day after his participation in the St Patrick's Day celebrations in Dublin.

In addition, someone's clothes can symbolise something, for example, a white wedding dress worn in a western Christian wedding symbolising the purity of the bride. Thus the clothes worn, and how, when and where they are worn can all be interpreted or discussed in terms of the messages they are trying to convey. Kringelbach (2007: 258–9), for example, discusses the importance of dress in relation to urban women's dancing in Senegal, she states:

> In Dakar, dressing well (*sañse*) and grooming the body are indeed unavoidable means of gaining status in the female world. When preparing for a dance event, women must find money for a new outfit, hairstyle and the latest fashionable underwear. There is a clear hierarchy of events, and this is particularly important for wedding and name-giving ceremonies. Moreover, married women are expected to dress more expensively than younger, unmarried women, as their elegance is assumed to be, at least in part, a reflection of their husbands' status.

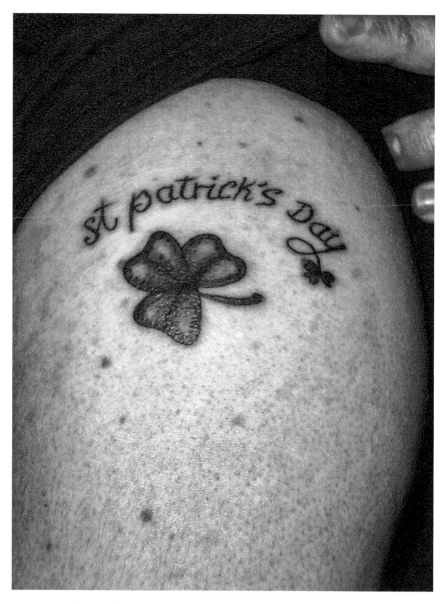

FIGURE 7.6 St Patrick's Day tattoo

Source: © Teresa Leopold.

The example from Senegal, the cosplay example and the Whitby Goth Festival all draw attention to different issues based on gender – the expected role of men and women and the role of women as the objects of a male gaze. We now want to discuss issues of gender in relation to events in more detail.

THINK POINT

Reflect on the attention that you give to your body and clothes before attending an event. Does this differ depending on the type of event and why?

Gender roles

We might identify ourselves as either male or female and these categories can be understood in relation to our biological functions of reproduction. However, the traits attributed to different genders are socially constructed. This means that understandings of what it is to be a woman or a man come from the social world. If we think back to chapter 2 and Geertz's (1973) analysis of the Balinese cockfight, the characteristics attributed to Balinese men symbolised in the cocks include strength and aggression. By contrast, women flight attendants, as discussed by Tyler and Hancock (2001), are seen to have the attributes of greater empathy, care and patience compared to men. We can see these sorts of gender distinctions manifest in flower shows, as Edwards (2011: 141) notes of the Gympie Horticultural Society in Australia:

> the first horticultural shows were more focused on the science of fruit and vegetable production, many men participated. When monthly shows were instituted, women came to dominate, as emphasis shifted towards flowers. Holmes (2006: 169) identified this as part of the gendered roles of gardening: 'women's gardening was more involved with creating beauty' than men's, which focus[es] on agricultural production.

Such gender stereotyping can be found elsewhere in different types of events. In addition if we link an examination of events to the wider social processes at play at the time an event takes place we can also see that they can mirror or reinforce prevailing social attitudes. We can therefore understand that gender stereotyping has been a feature of events for a long period of time. For example, Roche (2000) draws attention to the opposition of the American women's suffrage movement to the women's exhibition at the 1876 expo in Philadelphia. The items exhibited were drawn from the role of women in the family and foregrounded domestic crafts. The suffragettes' opposition was based on 'suspecting [the expo] of being likely to promote sexist stereotyping' (Roche 2000: 81). The fact that the women's movement were opposed to representation of women at the expo reiterates our earlier point (see chapter 6) that events can also be sites of resistance.

Some events are marked in a gendered way through the narratives attached to them. Wensing and Bruce (2003) discuss this through an analysis of media representations of gender during an international sporting event. They discuss how gender is a 'framing device' (Wensing and Bruce 2003: 287), which influences and reflects different attitudes to women's and men's participation in sporting events. If we consider the Wimbledon tennis tournament, the women's singles champion is paid less prize money than the male equivalent. It is argued that this is based on the women playing fewer sets because of their having less stamina. Nevertheless this would appear to undermine the woman's achievement.

THINK POINT

Examine the media coverage of men and women's participation in the same sporting event, for example, the Commonwealth Games. Identify how the football World Cups for men and women are portrayed in media.

CASE STUDY: NATIONALISM AND AMBIVALENCE – ETHNICITY, GENDER AND FOLKLORE AS CATEGORIES OF OTHERNESS

Israeli folk dance tradition was developed by a group of female Jewish immigrants from Europe to Palestine during the 1930s and 1940s. Dances were invented and formed based on Hebrew ceremonial festivals, and further developed with elements of Mizrahi Jews' and Arab ethnic dances, and are now considered authentically Israeli. In the mid 1940s, the first folk dance festival was organised, which continued until 1968 and was then substituted by the annual Carmiel Dance Festival, which is still held today. The early developments of these dance movement and dance traditions were exclusively led by women. However, over the last two decades there has been a fundamental shift in gender roles with largely male Mizrahi Jews taking control of the folklore movement by excluding Europeans, women and Arabs.

(*Source*: Roginsky 2006)

Summary

In this chapter we explored

- the concept of *habitus* and its importance in choices exercised with regard to events;
- the importance of all the senses to the experiential nature of events;
- the central role of the body and ideas of embodiment in understanding event practices;
- the relationship between events and gender stereotyping.

Suggested reading

Bourdieu, P. (1979) *Distinction: A Social Critique of the Judgement of Taste*. London: Routledge.

Featherstone, M., Hepworth, M. and Turner, B. (eds) (1991) *The Body: Social Process and Cultural Theory*. London: Sage.

Goulding, C. and Saren, M. (2009) 'Performing Identity: An Analysis of Gender Expressions at the Whitby Goth Festival', *Consumption Markets & Culture*, 12(1): 27–46.

Mauss, M. (1979) *Sociology and Psychology Essays*. London: Routledge and Kegan Paul.

Useful websites

Whitby Goth Festival: http://www.whitbygothweekend.co.uk
Viking Festivals Re-enactment:
http://www.vikingsofmiddleengland.co.uk/what_is_reenactment.html
Rio Carnival: http://www.rio-carnival.net
Royal Horticulture Society Events: http://www.rhs.org.uk/shows-events

Explanation for Figure 7.2

You were asked to interpret the event shown in Figure 7.2. The picture shows a float for the supermarket Safeway, which forms part of the 4 July Parade in Danville, California, USA, 2012.

8

CONCLUSION

This final chapter will reiterate the importance of taking a social science perspective when studying events to ensure that these occurrences are well understood and considered as socially and culturally rooted manifestations. We begin by retracing the main theoretical positions and concepts outlined in the preceding main six chapters of the book. Then we will consider briefly more ideas that are related to the study of events and that have not been covered in this book. We will suggest that, like the aspects covered in this book, these issues can also be further informed by taking a social science perspective to more fully understand their complexity and importance. We start by restating our argument that the study of events is enriched and more holistic by looking to what the disciplines of social science have to offer.

Why the social sciences?

Our starting point for the book was the identification of what we saw as a gap in the literature for events management studies. We felt that students were missing out on the wealth and richness of material and literature that serves to inform understandings and practices of events. We struggled with how the term 'events' was being interpreted, feeling it was too narrow. Our first task, then, was to broaden its application. We identified a number of terms in chapter 1 that have been used widely in social science research and writing but do not have such a strong presence in events management literature. In short, the events management literature, we feel, does not pay enough attention to the social and cultural embeddedness of these things it labels as 'events'.

Event research in its earlier stages was largely concerned with social science perspectives, such as the importance of events as part of a nation's customs and traditions (Palmer and Lloyd 1972) and the commercialisation of events and development of events due to social change (Wood 1982). However, in terms of the emergence of events as a discrete focus of study in the 1990s and early twenty-first century such social science perspectives have been overshadowed by a focus on events management (or been placed under the umbrella of events management) and instrumentalist business concerns. Although management insights are valuable to a business-driven approach they miss the wider social and cultural contexts in which events are practised (see e.g. Goldblatt 1997; Yeoman *et al.* 2004; Allen *et al.* 2008). The need to engage more fully with social science approaches to events has been acknowledged. For example, Toohey and Veal's (2000) study of the Olympic Games introduces various ways in which the Games are produced in relation to their interaction with changing social and cultural environments. Indeed, Roche (2000), in his discussion of mega-events, argues that they are important for understanding structure, change and agency and are also relevant for comprehending processes of change in the modern world.

> The national and international 'ecology of great public events' . . . has helped to structure the (social) space and time dimensions of modernity at the national and the international levels. Spatially, mega-events uniquely, if transiently, identify particular urban and national places in the national, international and global spaces of media and tourist markets and the gaze of their consumers.
>
> (Roche 2000: 7)

While Roche (2000: xi) uses the term 'mega-events', we believe that the ideas he outlines – of the value of studying this kind of happening – can also be applied to more localised and personal scales and that all events:

> contain much about the construction of, and connections between, the cultural, the political and the economic in modern societies and in the contemporary order. To understand something about their origins, nature and development in modernity is to throw light on phenomena and processes within modernity which continue to influence us even when the lights of any particular event have been switched off and when 'the show' appears to be over.

In this book we have identified processes and relevant theories that enable us to gain a much deeper understanding not only of the social and cultural significance of events but also how events can help us to understand society and culture. At this juncture we would like to restate the aim of this book as an introductory text, which encourages students to explore for themselves the depth of the arguments and discussions relating to the events context and thus recognise the complexity of events, which cannot just be simply reduced to business functions or another area of management. We will now briefly revisit each chapter to summarise the main points.

Chapter 2 considers the social significance of events. We began by considering what is meant by the term 'society' and the relationship between the organising nature or structure and the role of the individual or agency. This relationship between structure and agency influences the way we behave. Next we looked at the different stages of societal development – pre-modern, modern and postmodern – and examined the different kinds of events for these eras. In particular, we looked at some of the key characteristics and processes associated with modernity that have influenced the development and practice of varying types of events. A key trend that was identified is the increase in the number of events in Europe (Boissevain 1992, 2008), which is echoed elsewhere in the western world. We introduced the theories of Durkheim (1933) and Tönnies (1957) to explain the changes in society from the pre-modern to the modern.

Chapter 3 brings the focus onto ritual to explore the cyclical nature of some events. By this we mean those activities that occur on a regular basis and at specific intervals, for example celebrations such as birthdays and religious ceremonies. We consider the classification of some rituals into various types of rites. We introduce the work of van Gennep (1960) on rituals as rites of passage, which discusses the role of rituals as markers of life's stages, for example an initiation ceremony. Many personal events such as weddings fall into the category of a rite that signals change. We then think about how Victor Turner (1969) developed van Gennep's ideas, identifying that all rites involve three distinct phases: a pre-liminal stage, a liminal stage – associated with *communitas* – and a post-liminal stage. Our discussion also noted that in following this series of steps, many rite-based rituals use pre-defined scripts and are often associated with particular objects (e.g. the Olympic torch). We note that much of the argument has a religious context. Religion is arguably less significant in modern societies compared to the pre-modern world but this does not diminish the value of examining events in the light of a discussion about ritual. Indeed, we identify the emergence of secular rituals. These follow similar kinds of codes of practice as religious rituals but are not underpinned by religion. The development of so-called secular rituals is often associated with trying to provide a sense of history and longevity and is therefore linked to invented traditions.

Chapter 4 highlights the importance of performance as an essential element to understanding event consumers, narratives and experiences. We explored the inclusive nature of the term 'performance' to demonstrate that events are essentially made up of different performances and actors, including the audience and the 'players'. We examined the event as a performance, noting that it follows a sequence of phases regardless of how long it might last (compare a traditional Christian wedding to the pilgrimage to Mecca). We looked at Schechner's (2003) functions of performance and how they relate to the event context. By doing this we highlighted that one event contains many different performances. Next we thought about the unplanned nature of some events that are embedded in the social and cultural spheres of everyday life, and how these can change depending on the context of action. This led us to think about the constant negotiation and communication between context, performers and audiences, which gives rise to different meanings associated with the event for the different parties involved in its practice and which, in turn, influences the behaviour of the various agents involved. To illustrate this we introduced Deighton's (1992) categories of performance. We note that all these performances are the products of society which in themselves rely on material culture and artefacts to be enacted. Finally, we highlighted the ways in which performances can be contested so that the prescribed meaning can be overturned.

Chapter 5 is about consumer society and the idea of the experience economy. Consumption is a theme that occurs in most chapters but we give particular focus to it in this chapter. We begin by defining consumption and noting its application outside of purely economic concerns. An event can be an item for consumption but, at the same time, a single event can be composed of different elements that can be consumed in their own right, for example a can of drink and the clothes worn. Associated with consumer culture is the idea of commodification, which relates to material and non-material cultural products and experiences being assigned a monetary value in the market place. This brings us face to face with issues of authenticity and arguments about the erosion of cultural traditions. We go on to think about the symbolic value of the things that we consume and how these can be interpreted as expressions of who we are. If we accept that events are commodities then the consumption practices exercised in relation to events work as markers of distinction between self and others and can tell us something about identity. In terms of the experience economy, we examined how the search for sensation also forms part of the products of consumption but relies on experiences rather than goods. This allows us to focus on the emotive and embodied experience of events. The final issue looked at in the chapter acts to counterbalance a focus on consumption as not all events have this as a central concern. Thus we focus on giving, which enables us to consider the role of those events arranged for charitable, non-commercial fundraising and sponsorship.

Chapter 6 explores the importance of place and representation in the making of events. We consider the different meanings of space and place as well as the concept of landscape, and note the different disciplinary approaches to these seemingly everyday but rather complex terms. We go on to note the importance of a sense of place to the shaping of relations with, and experiences of, different physical contexts. This feeds into feelings of belonging and identification with places, and how these notions influence the form, participation and experiences in or with events. This can act to include as well as exclude people from events. To understand the interrelationship between different elements of space we use Lefebvre's (1991) writings on the productions of space. The three aspects he identifies are: spatial practices, representation of space and, not to be confused with the latter, representational space. A key point to note from this theory is that there is a relationship between the way a space is represented and how people behave in relation to these representations. Thus how the space is practised can either uphold or resist the representations. A dominant influence in the representation of space is the media and we briefly outline the role it can play in constructing narratives of events.

Chapter 7 discusses three key elements that help us to understand the practices and experiential nature of events; these are *habitus*, the body and gender. While these are three distinct and very large topics in their own right within the social sciences, we feel that they can be seen to interconnect with each other. We examined the concept of *habitus* to further understand the relationship between structure and agency by noting how our upbringing and surroundings influence our way of being in the world, helping to govern tastes, choices and actions. We apply this to events by thinking about how motives for participating in events are influenced by these underlying factors. Of central importance to the concept of *habitus* is concern with the ways in which the body is used, thus we go on to discuss the role of the senses and ideas of embodiment in helping to construct experiences of events. Here we refer to the way our bodies are who we are. We can understand this further by thinking about the example of cosplay in that the costumes worn and the ways in which the players use their bodies to re-enact the practices of the characters enables them to take on (or embody) the identity of the character they are playing – through the use of the body the participants know what it feels like to be a particular character. We should also remember that the body can be understood as a symbol, thus how it is used and how it is adorned can be interpreted in terms of the meanings in gestures, body markings and clothes. A recurring theme in the chapter's case studies and discussion is the role of women. This brought us to focus on gender and events. What the examples encountered seem to be telling us is that women are still often cast in stereotypical gender roles and are often still subjected to patriarchal hegemony.

As with any book, the themes identified reflect the interests of the authors. We fully recognise therefore that what we have included in the book necessarily excludes much else of possible interest in this context. However it was never our intention to mine every area or theory in the social sciences but rather to highlight some issues, which we believe are fundamental to the study of events. We now wish to turn to consider what could be covered in a second volume, which include issues of volunteering and social capital, race and ethnicity, technology, globalisation, access, sustainability and the green consumer as well as the role of the informal economy in events.

Areas for further research

Volunteering

Volunteering at events has received a fair amount of attention in academic literature and is considered as essential for many events to take place, with some activities relying on large numbers of volunteers. For example, the Olympics in London in 2012 worked with 70,000 volunteers, who were called Games Makers (London 2012). As this name suggests, volunteers are seen as essential to the success of an event. Many charities in the UK are now working closely with universities' events management programmes to ensure a steady stream of volunteers, provide work experiences for students and encourage the organisation of student-led fundraising events. Existing research on the study of event volunteers has focused on a range of different issues such as motivations (e.g. Monga 2006), recruitment and retention of volunteers (e.g. Coyne and Coyne 2001; Fairley *et al.* 2007), volunteer demographics (e.g. Saleh and Wood 1998) and gender differentiation (e.g. Downward *et al.* 2005). It is not our intention here to explore the issue in depth, however we would like to highlight that a second volume of this book could include a focus on the notion of social capital. This is not a new approach within the study of events (see for example Arcodia and Whitford 2007) but would provide a strong social science approach to more fully understand the complexity and importance of the issue.

More on socialisation

Our discussion of *habitus* in chapter 7 of this volume provides social science informed considerations that highlight how a person's social background and the values attributed to her or his tastes inform her or his actions and dispositions. We drew out the issue of gender constructions as an element of socialisation processes that could influence engagement with events. We could have focused on race, ethnicity, religion and class as factors that affect individual or group interaction with events. Studies of race and ethnicity can provide us with a critical understanding of the issues of the social construction of events, ideas of belonging, concerns of social inclusion and exclusion and underlying political notions that exist in the events' context. For example, Spiropoulos *et al.*'s (2006) focus on the ethnicity of the various stakeholders at the Greek Festival in Sydney provides insights into how ethnicity influences managerial issues and has implications for the organisation and running of the festival.

Technology and social media

Advances in technology and social media are impacting on many aspects of the events industry and indeed our daily lives. With a shift to bottom-up rather than top-down knowledge production, much of our knowledge and information is now available through technical resources such as Wikipedia, rather than more traditional paper-based forms of information dissemination. We mentioned before that events are social happenings so that the development of technology – particularly given the rate at which it is currently being advanced through new gadgets and improved versions of technical equipment – means we need to engage with studies that help us understand people's interactions with this ever developing field. The idea here is that we move beyond looking at what technology can enable us to do, for example through electronic name signs at conferences and events held in Second Life, and ask how technology influences us as a society – particularly as technology is developing at a rate faster than our understandings of its impacts on us. We now live in an 'infosphere' meaning that information received through technological gadgets has become part of the environment for a vast majority of people. Just consider how often you interact with friends and family through technological tools rather than talking to a person next to you. Thus we need to question how the information revolution is affecting our understanding of ourselves (as agents) (Floridi 2010).

Globalisation

While we have touched upon the issue of globalisation in our discussion of modernity and postmodernity in chapter 2, we suggest that the complexity of this topic allows for a much more focused and in-depth discussion within the context of social science and events. Fox Gotham (2005: 309) highlights that 'the notion of globalisation involves several issues, including whether changing connections between the global and the local entails increasing cultural homogeneity or increasing heterogeneity or a mixture of both'. In other words, we have to question how globalisation impacts on issues such as place and community attachment, tradition, a feeling of belonging, ethnicity and heritage. This book has introduced a number of social science approaches which are crucial to these discussions, such as place, the construction of space and issues of consumption; but we feel that the importance and relevance of globalisation today justifies a more fully developed analysis of the topic.

Economies of events

Another area of study is economic approaches within the event context, which move beyond seeing events as commercial transactions and focusing on the economic impact of events. In other words, a focus on informal and alternative economies would allow us to move beyond seeing the economy as the driving factor of events but consider the 'multifarious social exchanges that do not follow the "rules" of a capitalist market economy' (Mosedale 2011: 195). Just consider informal economic activities that take place within the event context, such as black market ticket sales and potentially unregistered sales of merchandise (see Figure 8.1).

In addition to focusing on these different forms of economy, we suggest that the study of economy for events needs to consider elements such as culture and politics. In particular politics, in conjunction with studies of *political economy*, is an area that would enhance the understanding of events, as it would allow discussion to move beyond policies and political structures to issues of power and control.

Sustainability

Finally, the issue of sustainability has been discussed more widely within the events management literature than other topics that we have thus far suggested. However, we believe that this discussion needs to be enhanced through concepts such as 'contested natures' (Macnaghten and Urry 1998), and questions relating to what we mean by 'nature' (e.g. Soper 1995), governance and sustainable livelihoods to

FIGURE 8.1 Sale of flags during Olympic Relay, UK, 2012

Source: © Les Roberts.

provide a more critical view. Aligning with this, we suggest that the discussion on consumption needs to be broadened to include the idea of the 'green consumer' and the link to green consumerism. By this we mean consumption behaviour, which reflects an awareness of 'the effects of manufacturing and consumption on the natural environment' (Wagner 1997: 1). Thus, for this last suggestion, we mirror Gilg *et al*.'s (2005: 481) argument that 'green buying must be seen in the context of wider debates surrounding the development of sustainable ways of living that incorporate other environmental actions in an holistic conceptualisation of sustainable lifestyles'.

With this book we would like to encourage and challenge students to become aware of the complex nature of events, to consider what events actually are and the necessity of studying the socio-cultural context in which they are practised. In so doing, we advocate engagement with a range of social science theories, literature and associated terminology. The topics suggested for inclusion in a future volume, like the book as a whole are not exhaustive. Indeed, the more we probe the more we find that could be brought to the table of events management studies. The theories and issues that the intellectually curious scholar could continue to discover would not only enhance and enrich the study of these things labelled events but would also allow what are truly human endeavours and activities to be revealed for what they tell us about people and what people tell us about events.

BIBLIOGRAPHY

Abram, S. (1996) 'Performing for Tourists in Rural France', in S. Abram, J. Waldren and D. Macleod (eds) *Tourists and Tourism: Identifying with People and Places*. Oxford: Berg, 29–49.

Allain, P. and Harvie, J. (2006) *The Routledge Companion to Theatre and Performance*. London: Routledge.

Allen, J., O'Toole, W., Harris, R. and McDonnell, I. (2008) *Festival and Special Event Management*, 4th edn. Milton, Qld: Wiley Australia.

Andrews, H. (2009) 'Tourism as a Moment of Being', *Suomen Antropologi*, 34(2): 5–21.

Andrews, H. and Roberts, L. (eds) (2012) *Liminal Landscapes: Travel, Experience and Spaces In-between*, London: Routledge.

Arcodia, C. and Whitford, M. (2007) 'Festival Attendance and the Development of Social Capital', *Journal of Convention & Event Tourism*, 8(2): 1–18.

Arnold, R. (2006) *Thailand Phi-Phi Tsunami Dive Camp*, http://phi-phitsunamidivecamp. blogspot.com/ (accessed April 2007).

Atkinson, D. and Laurier, E. (1998) 'A Sanitised City? Social Exclusion at Bristol's 1996 International Festival of the Sea', *Geoforum*, 29(2): 199–206.

Barnett, J. (1949) 'The Easter Festival – A Study in Cultural Change', *American Sociological Review*, 14(1): 62–70.

Baudrillard, J. (1995) *The Gulf War Did Not Take Place*. Bloomington: Indiana University Press.

Bauman, R. and Briggs, C. (1990) 'Poetics and Performance as Critical Perspectives on Language and Social Life', *Annual Review of Anthropology*, 19: 59–88.

Bennett, R., Mousley, W., Kitchin, P. and Ali-Choudhury, R. (2007) 'Motivations for Participating in Charity-affiliated Sporting Events', *Journal of Customer Behaviour*, 6(2): 155–78.

Bocock, R. (1993) *Consumption*. London: Routledge.

Boissevain, J. (1992) *Revitalizing European Rituals*. London: Routledge.

Boissevain, J. (ed.) (1996) *Coping with Tourists: European Reactions to Mass Tourism*. Oxford: Berghahn.

Boissevain, J. (2008) 'Some Notes on Tourism and the Revitalisation of Calendrical Festivals in Europe', *Journal of Mediterranean Studies*, 18(1): 17–41.

Bourdieu, P. (1977) *Outline of a Theory of Practice*, Cambridge: Cambridge University Press.

Bourdieu, P. (1979) *Distinction: A Social Critique of the Judgement of Taste*. London: Routledge.

Bourdieu, P. (1990) *The Logic of Practice*, Cambridge: Polity.

Britton, S. (1991) 'Tourism, Capital and Place: Towards a Critical Geography of Tourism', *Environment and Planning D*, 9: 451–78.

Brown, S. and James, J. (2004) 'Event Design and Management: Ritual Sacrifice?', in I. Yeoman, M. Robertson, J. Ali-Knight, S. Drummond and U. McMahon-Beattie (eds) *Festival and Events Management: An International Arts and Culture Perspective*. Oxford: Butterworth Heinemann.

Carú, A. and Cova, B. (2003) 'Revisiting Consumption Experience: A More Humble But Complete View of the Concept', *Marketing Theory*, 3: 267–86.

Chang, W. and Yuan, J. (2011) 'A Taste of Tourism: Visitors' Motivations to Attend a Food Festival', *Event Management*, 15: 13–23.

Clawson, M. and Knetsch, J. (1966) *Economics of Outdoor Recreation*. Baltimore, MD: Johns Hopkins University Press.

Cleaver M., Green B. and Muller T. (2000) 'Using Consumer Behaviour Research to Understand the Baby Boomer Tourist', *Journal of Hospitality and Tourism Research*, 24(2): 274–87.

Cohen, A. (1982) 'A Polyethnic London Carnival as a Contested Cultural Performance', *Ethnic and Racial Studies*, 5(1): 23–41.

Cole, T. (2003) 'Turning the Places of Holocaust History into Places of Holocaust Memory', in S. Hornstein and F. Jacobowitz (eds) *Image and Remembrance: Representation and the Holocaust*. Bloomington: Indiana University Press.

Cosman, M.P. (1984) *Medieval Holidays and Festivals – A Calendar of Celebrations*. London: Judy Piatkus.

Costa, X. (2002) 'Festive Identity: Personal and Collective Identity in the Fire Carnival of the "Fallas" (València, Spain)', *Social Identities: Journal for the Study of Race, Nation and Culture*, 8(2): 321–45.

Coyne, B. and Coyne, E. (2001) 'Getting, Keeping and Caring for Unpaid Volunteers for Professional Golf Tournament Events', *Human Resource Development International*, 4(2): 199–216.

Crehan, K. (2011) *Community Art: An Anthropological Perspective*. Oxford: Berg.

Crompton, J. and McKay, S. (1997) 'Motives of Visitors attending Festival Events', *Annals of Tourism Research*, 24(2): 425–39.

Crouch, D. (1999) 'The Intimacy and Expansion of Space', in D. Crouch (ed.) *Leisure/Tourism: Geographies, Practices and Heographical Knowledge*. London: Routledge.

Cruces, F. and Díaz de Rada, A. (1992) 'Public Celebrations in a Spanish Valley', in J. Boissevain (ed.) *Revitalising European Rituals*. London: Routledge, 62–79.

Cunningham, S., Cornwell, B. and Coote, L. (2009) 'Expressing Identity and Shaping Image: The Relationship Between Corporate Mission and Corporate Sponsorship', *Journal of Sport Management*, 23: 65–86.

Datta, V. (1993) 'A Bohemian Festival: La Fête de la Vache Enragée', *Journal of Contemporary History*, 28(2): 195–213.

Dayan, D. and Katz, E. (1987) 'Performing Media Events', in J. Curran, A. Smith and P. Wingate (eds) *Impacts and Influences: Essays on Media Power in the Twentieth Century*. London: Methuen.

Dayan, D. and Katz, E. (1988) 'Articulating Consensus: The Ritual and Rhetoric of Media Events', in J. Alexander (ed.) *Durkheimian Sociology*. Cambridge: Cambridge University Press.

Dayan, D. and Katz, E. (1992) *Media Events*. London: Harvard University Press.

Deighton, J. (1992) 'The Consumption of Performance', *Journal of Consumer Research*, 19(3): 362–72.

Derrett, R. (2003) 'Making Sense of How Festivals Demonstrate a Community's Sense of Place', *Event Management*, 8(1): 48–58.

Douglas, M. (1996) *Thought Styles: Critical Essays on Good Taste*. London: Sage.

Downward, P. and Ralston, R. (2006) 'The Sports Development Potential of Sports Event Volunteering: Insights from the XVII Manchester Commonwealth Games', *European Sport Management Quarterly*, 6(4): 333–51.

Duffy, M. (2009) *Music of Place*. Saarbrüchen: Verlag Dr Müller.

Duffy, M. and Waitt, G. (2011) 'Rural Festivals and Processes of Belonging', in C. Gibson and J. Connell (eds) *Festival Places: Revitalising Rural Australia*. Bristol: Channel View, 44–57.

Durkheim, E. (1915) *The Elementary Forms of the Religious Life*. London: George Allen and Unwin.

Durkheim, E. (1933) *The Division of Labour in Society*. London: Macmillan.

Edwards, R. (2011) 'Birthday Parties and Flower Shows, Musters and Multiculturalism: Festivals in Post-war Gympie', in C. Gibson and J. Connell (eds) *Festival Places: Revitalising Rural Australia*. Bristol: Channel View, 136–54.

Enloe, C. (2000) *Manoeuvres: The International Politics of Militarizing Women's Lives*. Berkeley: University of California Press.

European Commission (2009) *European Capitals of Culture: The Road to Success – From 1985 to 2010*. Luxembourg: Office for Official Publications of the European Communities.

Fairley, S., Kellett, P. and Green, B. (2007) 'Volunteering Abroad: Motives for Travel to Volunteer at the Athens Olympic Games', *Journal of Sport Management*, 21(1): 41–57.

Falassi, A. (1987) 'Festival: Definition and Morphology', in A. Falassi (ed.) *Time Out of Time: Essays on the Festival*. Albuquerque, NM: University of New Mexico Press, 1–10.

Falk, P. (1994) *The Consuming Body*. London: Sage.

Featherstone, M. (1991) 'The Body in Consumer Culture', in M. Featherstone, M. Hepworth and B. Turner (eds) *The Body: Social Process and Cultural Theory*. London: Sage, 170–96.

Featherstone, M., Hepworth, M. and Turner, B. (eds) (1991) *The Body: Social Process and Cultural Theory*. London: Sage.

Filo, K., Funk, D. and O'Brien, D. (2009) 'The Meaning Behind Attachment: Exploring Camaraderie, Cause, and Competency at a Charity Sport Event', *Journal of Sport Management* 23: 361–87.

Floridi, L. (2010) 'The Philosophy of Information as a Conceptual Framework', *Knowledge, Technology & Policy*, 23(1–2): 253–81.

Fortier, M. (1999) 'Re-membering Places and the Performance of Belonging(s)', special issue on Performativity and Belonging', *Theory, Culture &Society*, 16(2): 41–64.

Foucault, M. (1976) *The Birth of the Clinic*. London: Tavistock.

Foucault, M. (1977) *Discipline and Punish: The Birth of the Prison*. Harmondsworth: Penguin.

Fournier, L.S. (2007) 'Traditional Games and the Ritual Year in Provence (France): From Ludodiversity to Cultural Heritage', in *The Ritual Year and Ritual Diversity*, Proceedings from the International Conference of the SIEF Working Group on the Ritual Year. Gothenburg, Sweden, 7–11 June 2006, 183–90.

Friedman, J. (1994) *Consumption and Identity*. Australia: Harwood Academic Publishers.

Fulcher, J. and Scott, J. (2007) *Sociology*. Oxford: Oxford University Press.

Galt, A. (1973) 'Carnival on the Island of Pantelleria: Ritualized Community Solidarity in an Atomistic Society', *Ethnology*, 12(3): 325–39.

Geertz, C. (1973) *The Interpretation of Cultures*. New York: Basic Books.

Gell, A. (1996) 'Reflections on a Cut Finger: Taboo in the Umeda Conception of the Self', in M. Jackson (ed.) *Things as They Are: New Directions in Phenomenological Anthropology*. Bloomington: Indiana University Press, 115–127.

Getz, D. (2007) *Event Studies: Theory, Research and Policy for Planned Events*, 1st edn. Oxford: Butterworth Heinemann.

Getz, D. (2012) *Event Studies: Theory, Research and Policy for Planned Events*, 2nd edn. Abingdon: Routledge.

Getz, D. and Cheyne, J. (2002) 'Special Event Motives and Behaviour', in C. Ryan (ed.) *The Tourist Experience*. London: Thomson.

Gibson, C. and Connell, J. (eds) (2011) *Festival Places: Revitalising Rural Australia*. Bristol: Channel View.

Gibson, C., Connell, J., Waitt, G. and Walmsley, J. (2011) 'The Extent and Significance of Rural Festivals', in C. Gibson and J. Connell (eds) (2011) *Festival Places: Revitalising Rural Australia*. Bristol: Channel View.

Gilg, A., Barr, S. and Ford, N. (2005) 'Green Consumption or Sustainable Lifestyles? Identifying the Sustainable Consumer', *Futures*, 37(6): 481–504.

Gilmore, D. (1993) 'The Democratization of Ritual: Andalusian Carnival after Franco', *Anthropological Quarterly*, 66(1): 37–47.

Glazer, A. and Konrad, K. (1996) 'A Signaling Explanation for Charity', *American Economic Review*, 86(4): 1019–28.

Goffman, E. (1959) *The Presentation of the Self in Everyday Life*. Harmondsworth: Penguin.

Goldblatt, J. (1997) *Special Events: Best Practices in Modern Event Management*, 2nd edn. New Jersey: Van Nostrand Reinhold.

Gotham, K.F. (2005) 'Tourism from Above and Below: Globalization, Localization and New Orleans's Mardi Gras', *International Journal of Urban and Regional Research*, 29(2): 309–26.

Goulding, C. and Saren, M. (2009) 'Performing Identity: An Analysis of Gender Expressions at the Whitby Goth Festival', *Consumption Markets & Culture*, 12(1): 27–46.

Gray, J. (2003) 'Open Spaces and Dwelling Places: Being at Home on Hill Farms in the Scottish Borders', in S. Low and D. Lawrence-Zuniga (eds) *The Anthropology of Space and Place: Locating Culture*. Oxford: Blackwell, 224–44.

Green, G. (2007) '"Come to Life": Authenticity, Value, and the Carnival as Cultural Commodity in Trinidad and Tobago', *Identities: Global Studies in Culture and Power*, 14(1–2): 203–24.

Greenwood, D. (1989) 'Culture by the Pound: An Anthropological Perspective on Tourism as Cultural Commoditisation', in V. Smith (ed.) *Hosts and Guests: The Anthropology of Tourism*, 2nd edn. Oxford: Blackwell.

Guiu, C. (2008) 'Ritual Revitalization and the Construction of Places in Catalonia, Spain', *Journal of Mediterranean Studies*, 18(1): 93–118.

Gunnell, T. (2007) '*Busar*: Initiation Traditions in Icelandic Gymnasia', in *The Ritual Year and Ritual Diversity*, Proceedings from the International Conference of the SIEF Working Group on the Ritual Year, Gothenburg, Sweden, 7–11 June 2006, 287–97.

Guttmann, A. (2002) *The Olympics: A History of the Modern Games*. Urbana and Chicago: University of Illinois Press.

Hagström, C. (2007) 'To Create a Sense of Belongings: Christening Gifts as Materialization of Feelings', in *The Ritual Year and Ritual Diversity*, Proceedings from the International Conference of the SIEF Working Group on the Ritual Year, Gothenburg, Sweden, 7–11 June 2006, 142–6.

Hall, S. and Jefferson, T. (2006) *Resistance through Rituals: Youth Subcultures in Post-war Britain*. London and New York: Routledge.

Handelman, D. (1998) *Models and Mirrors: Towards an Anthropology of Public Events*. Oxford: Berghahn.

Harris, R. and Huyskens, M. (2001) 'Research Note. Events Beyond 2000: Setting the Agenda – Focus Group Outcomes', *Events Management*, 6: 271–72.

Hi Phi Phi (Help International Phi Phi) (2005) 'Return to Paradise Carnival', Hi Phi Phi, http://www.hiphiphi.com/press.htm (accessed March 2007).

Henderson, G. (2009) 'Placelessness', in D. Gregory, R. Johnston, G. Pratt, M. Watts and S. Whatmore (eds) *The Dictionary of Human Geography*. Chichester: Wiley-Blackwell, 542.

Higham, J. and Ritchie, B. (2001) 'The Evolution of Festivals and other Events in Rural Southern New Zealand', *Event Management*, 7: 39–49.

Hindle, S. (1995) 'Custom, Festival and Protest in Early Modern England: The Little Budworth Wakes, St Peter's Day, 1596', *Rural History*, 6(2): 155–78.

Hirsch, E. and O'Hanlon, M. (1995) *The Anthropology of Landscape: Perspectives on Place and Space*. Oxford: Clarendon Press.

Hobsbawm, E. and Ranger, T. (1983) *The Invention of Tradition*. Cambridge: Cambridge University Press.

Holbrook, M. and Hirschman, E. (1982) 'The Experiential Aspects of Consumption: Consumer Fantasies, Feelings, and Fun', *Journal of Consumer Research*, 9(2): 132–40.

Hornstein, S. (2003) 'Invisible Topographies', in S. Hornstein and F. Jacobowitz (eds) *Image and Remembrance: Representation and the Holocaust*. Bloomington: Indiana University Press.

Hulse, T. (1997) 'Saint Winifred's Well: A Journey of Healing and Renewal', in J. Westwood (ed.) *Sacred Journeys: Paths for the New Pilgrim*. London: Gaia Books, 186–87.

Jackson, M. (1989) *Paths Toward a Clearing: Radical Empiricism and Ethnographic Inquiry*. Bloomington: Indiana University Press.

Jackson, M. (2005) *Existential Anthropology: Events, Exigencies and Effects*. Oxford: Berghahn.

Jackson. P. (1993) 'Towards a Cultural Politics of Consumption', in J. Bird, B. Curtis, T. Putnam, G. Robertson and L. Tickner (eds) *Mapping the Futures: Local Cultures, Global Change*. London: Routledge, 207–28.

Jago, L. and Shaw, R. (1998) 'Special Events: A Conceptual and Definitional Framework', *Festival Management & Event Tourism*, 5: 21–32.

Janiskee, B. (1980) 'South Carolina's Harvest Festivals: Rural Delights for Day Tripping Urbanites', *Journal of Cultural Geography*, 1(1): 96–104.

Kates, S. (2003) 'Producing and Consuming Gendered Representations: An Interpretation of the Sydney Gay and Lesbian Mardi Gras', *Consumption Markets & Culture*, 6(1): 5–22.

Kirkup, N. (2012) 'Olympic Tourist: Seeking a Sense of Belonging and the Construction of Social Identities', in R. Shipway and A. Fyall (eds) *International Sport Events – Impacts, Experiences and Identities*. Abingdon: Routledge.

Klausen, A. (1999a) 'Norwegian Culture and Olympism: Confrontations and Adaptations', in A. Klausen (ed.) *Olympic Games as Performance and Public Event. The Case of the XVII Winter Olympic Games in Norway*. Oxford: Berghahn Books, 27–48.

Klausen, A. (1999b) 'The Torch Relay: Reinvention of Tradition and Conflict with the Greeks', in A. Klausen (ed.) *Olympic Games as Performance and Public Event: The Case of the XVII Winter Olympic Games in Norway*. Oxford: Berghahn, 75–95.

Klausen, A. (ed.) (1999c) *Olympic Games as Performance and Public Event. The Case of the XVII Winter Olympic Games in Norway*. Oxford: Berghahn.

Knox, D. and Hannam, K. (2007) 'Embodying Everyday Masculinities in Heritage Tourism(s)', in A. Pritchard, N. Morgan, I. Ateljevic and C. Harris (eds) *Tourism and Gender: Embodiment, Sensuality and Experience*. Wallingford: CABI Publishing.

Knuts, E. (2007) 'Wedding Markets – Seasons for Sale', in *The Ritual Year and Ritual Diversity*, Proceedings from the International Conference of the SIEF Working Group on the Ritual Year, Gothenburg, Sweden, 7–11 June 2006, 147–54.

Kooistra, S. (2011) 'Festivalganger wil intimiteit', *De Volkskrant*, 13 August: 19.

Kover, A.I. (2001) 'The Sponsorship Issue', *Journal of Advertising Research*, 41: 5–15.

Kringelbach, H. (2007) '"Cool Play": Emotionality and Dance as a Resource in Senegalese Urban Women's Associations', in H. Wulff (ed.) *The Emotions: A Cultural Reader*. Oxford: Berg, 251–72.

Krom, M. (2008) 'Festivals of Moors and Christians: Performance, Commodity and Identity in Folk Celebrations in Southern Spain', *Journal of Mediterranean Studies*, 18(1): 119–38.

Kuutma, K. (1998) 'Festival as Communicative Performance and Celebration of Ethnicity', *Folklore: Electronic Journal of Folklore*, 7: 79–86 (print version) or 1–5 (e-version).

Lawton, J. and Weaver, D. (2010) 'Normative and Innovative Sustainable Resource Management at Birding Festivals', *Tourism Management*, 31(4): 527–36.

Lefebvre, H. (1991) *The Production of Space*. Oxford: Blackwell.

Lewis, C. and Pile, S. (1996) 'Woman, Body, Space: Rio Carnival and the Politics of Performance', *Gender, Place and Culture*, 3(1): 23–41.

Lloyd, F. (1993) *Deconstructing Madonna*. London: Batsford.

London 2012 (2012) 'Volunteers', London 2012 Olympics, http://www.london2012.com/about-us/volunteers/ (accessed June 2012).

Longhurst, B. and Savage, M (1996) 'Social Class, Consumption and the Influence of Bourdieu: Some Critical Issues', in S. Edgell *et al.* (eds) *Consumption Matters*, Oxford: Blackwell.

Low, S. and Lawrence-Zúñiga, D. (eds) (2003) *The Anthropology of Space and Place: Locating Culture*. Oxford: Blackwell.

MacCannell, D. (1976) *The Tourist: A New Theory of the Leisure of the Class*. London: Macmillan.

MacLeod, N. (2006) 'The Placeless Festival: Identity and Place in the Post-modern Festival', in D. Picard and M. Robinson (eds) *Festivals, Tourism and Social Change*. Clevedon: Channel View Publications.

Macnaghten, P. and Urry, J. (1998) *Contested Natures*. London: Sage.

Massey, D. and Jess, P. (1995) *A Place in the World?* Oxford: Oxford University Press.

Mauss, M. (1979) *Sociology and Psychology Essays*. London: Routledge and Keegan Paul.

Mayes, R. (2011) 'On Display: Ravensthorpe Wildflower Show and the Assembly of Place', in C. Gibson and J. Connell (eds) *Festival Places: Revitalising Rural Australia*. Bristol: Channel View, 155–71.

McDonnell, I. (2003) 'Events', in J. Jenkins and J. Pigram (eds) *Encyclopedia of Leisure and Outdoor Recreation*. London: Routledge, 163–6.

McIntosh, R. and Goeldner, C. (1986) *Tourism Principles: Practices and Philosophies*. New York: Wiley.

Meethan, K. (2001) *Tourism and Global Society*. Basingstoke: Palgrave.

Miller, D. (1995) 'Consumption Studies as the Transformation of Anthropology', in D. Miller (ed.) *Acknowledging Consumption: A Review of New Studies*. London: Routledge, 264–95.

Millward, P. (2009) 'Glasgow Rangers Supporters in the City of Manchester: The Degeneration of a "Fan Party" into a "Hooligan Riot', *International Review for the Sociology of Sport*, 44(4): 381–98.

Milne, S. (1998) 'Tourism and Sustainable Development: Exploring the Global–Local Nexus', in C. Hall and A. Lew (eds) *Sustainable Tourism: A Geographical Perspective*. New York: Longman, 35–48.

Mitchell, J. and Armstrong, G. (2005) 'Cheers and Booze: Football and *Festa* Drinking in Malta', in T. Wilson (ed.) *Drinking Cultures*. Oxford: Berg.

Monga, M. (2006) 'Measuring Motivation to Volunteer for Special Events', *Event Management*, 10(1): 47–61.

Moore, S. and Myerhoff, B. (eds) (1977) *Secular Ritual*. Amsterdam: Van Gorcum.

Morgan, M., Elbe, J. and de Esteban Curiel, J. (2009) 'Has the Experience Economy Arrived? The Views of Destination Managers in Three Visitor-dependent Areas', *International Journal of Tourism Research*, 11: 201–16.

Morton, C (2011) 'When Bare Breasts Are a "Threat": The Production of Bodies/Spaces in Law', *Canadian Journal of Women and the Law*, 23(2): 601–26.

Mosedale, J. (2011) 'Thinking Outside the Box: Alternative Political Economies in Tourism', in J. Mosedale (ed.) *Political Economy of Tourism: A Critical Perspective*. London: Routledge, 93–108.

Mosse, G. (1971) 'Caesarism, Circuses, and Monuments', *Journal of Contemporary History*, 6(2): 167–82.

Ohrvik, A. (2007) 'Ritualization as Entrepreneurship', in *The Ritual Year and Ritual Diversity*, Proceedings from the International Conference of the SIEF Working Group on the Ritual Year, Gothenburg, Sweden, 7–11 June, 103–8.

Ozaki, R. and Lewis, J. (2006) 'Boundaries and the Meaning of Social Space: A Study of Japanese House Plans', *Environment and Planning D: Society and Space*, 24: 91–104.

Palmer, G. and Lloyd, N. (1972) *A Year of Festivals: A Guide to British Calendar Customs*. London: F. Warne.

Pearce, D. G. (1995) *Tourism Today: A Geographical Analysis*, 2nd edn. Harlow: Longman.

Philo, G. and Berry, M. (2004) *Bad News from Israel*. London. Pluto Press

Phipps, P. (2011) 'Performing Culture as Political Strategy: The Garma Festival, Northeast Arnhem Land', in C. Gibson and J. Connell (eds) *Festival Places: Revitalising Rural Australia*. Bristol: Channel View, 109–22.

Phuket Press Center (2005a) 'General Information on the "One Year in Memory of Tsunami"' Ceremony', Phuket Press Center, Phuket, December.

Phuket Press Center (2005b) 'The "One Year in Memory of Tsunami" Ceremony', Phuket Press Center, Phuket, December.

Pine, J. and Gilmore, J. (1998) 'Welcome to the Experience Economy', *Harvard Business Review*, July–August: 97–105.

Pine, J. and Gilmore, J. (1999) *The Experience Economy: Work is Theatre and Every Business a Stage*. Boston, MA: Harvard Business School Press.

Poppi, C. (1992) 'Building Difference: The Political Economy of Tradition in the Ladin Carnival of the Val di Fassa', in J. Boissevain (ed.) *Revitalising European Rituals*. London: Routledge, 113–36.

Pritchard, A. and Jaworski, A. (2005) 'Introduction: Discourse, Communication and Tourism Dialogues', in A. Jaworski and A. Pritchard (eds) *Discourse, Communication and Tourism*. Clevedon: Channel View Publications.

Puijk, R. (1999) 'Producing Norwegian Culture for Domestic and Foreign Gazes: The Lillehammer Olympic Opening Ceremony', in A. Klausen (ed.) *Olympic Games as Performance and Public Event: The Case of the XVII Winter Olympic Games in Norway*. New York: Berghahn, 97–136.

Real, M. (1989) *Super Media: A Cultural Studies Approach*. London: Sage.

Real, M. (1995) 'Sport and the Spectacle', in J. Downing, A. Mohammadi and A. Sreberny-Mohammadi (eds) *Questioning the Media*, 2nd edn. London: Sage.

Real, M. (1996a) *Exploring Media Culture*. London: Sage.

Real, M. (1996b) 'The Postmodern Olympics: Technology and the Commodification of the Olympic Movement', *Quest*, 48: 9–24.

Real, M. (1996c) 'Is Television Corrupting the Olympics? Media and the (Post) Modern Games at Age 100', *Television Quarterly*, summer: 2–12.

Real, M. (1996d) 'The Televised Olympics from Atlanta: A Look Back – And Ahead', *Television Quarterly* autumn: 9–12.

Real, M. (1998) 'Mediasport: Technology and the Commodification of Postmodern Sport', in L. Wenner (ed.) *MediaSport*. London: Routledge.

Roberts, L. (ed.) (2012) *Mapping Cultures: Place, Practice, Performance*. Basingstoke: Palgrave.

Robinson, M., Picard, D. and Long, P. (2004) 'Introduction – Festival Tourism: Producing, Translating, and Consuming Expressions of Culture(s)', *Event Management*, 8(4): 187–9.

Roche, M. (2000) *Mega-events and Modernity*. London: Routledge.

Roginsky, D. (2006) 'Nationalism and Ambivalence: Ethnicity, Gender and Folklore as Categories of Otherness', *Patterns of Prejudice*, 40(3): 237–258.

Saleh, F. and Wood, C. (1998) 'Motives of Volunteers in Multicultural Events: The Case of Saskatoon Folkfest', *Festival Management and Event Tourism*, 5(1–2): 59–70.

Sardar, Z. and Van Loon, B. (2000) *Introducing Media Studies*. Cambridge: Icon Books.

Savage, M., Bagnell, G. and Longhurst, B. (2005) *Globalization and Belonging*. London: Sage.

Schechner, R. (1988) *Performance Theory*, 1st edn. New York: Routledge

Schechner, R. (2003) *Performance Theory*, 2nd edn. New York: Routledge.

Schechner, R. (2006) *Performance Studies*. New York: Routledge.

Shields, R. (1999) *Lefebvre, Love and Struggle: Spatial Dialectics*. London: Routledge.

Solomon, M. (1983) 'The Role of Products as Social Stimuli: A Symbolic Interactionism Perspective', *Journal of Consumer Research*, 10(3): 319–29.

Soper, K. (1995) *What is Nature?* Oxford: Blackwell.

Spiropoulos, S., Gargalianos, D. and Sotiriadou, K. (2006) 'The 20th Greek Festival of Sydney: A Stakeholder Analysis', *Event Management*, 9: 169–83.

Stanley, D. (2007) 'Pilgrimage to the Sea. European Romani and the Festival of Saint Sara', in *The Ritual Year and Ritual Diversity*, Proceedings from the International Conference of the SIEF Working Group on the Ritual Year, Gothenburg, Sweden, 7–11 June 2006, 240–245.

Stevenson, T. and Alaug, A. (2000) 'Football in Newly United Yemen: Rituals of Equity, Identity, and State Formation', *Journal of Anthropological Research*, 56(4): 453–75.

Tenfelde, K. (1978) 'Mining Festivals in the Nineteenth Century', special issue on Workers' Culture, *Journal of Contemporary History*, 13(2): 377–412.

Thomassen, B. (2009) 'Uses and Meanings of Liminality', *International Political Anthropology*, 2(1): 5–28.

Thomassen, B. (2012) 'Revisiting Liminality: The Danger of Empty Spaces', in H. Andrews and L. Roberts (eds) *Liminal Landscapes: Travel, Experience and Spaces In-between*. London: Routledge, 21–35.

Thompson, J. (1991) 'Editor's Introduction', in P. Bourdieu, *Language and Symbolic Power*, Cambridge: Polity Press.

Tönnies, F. (1957) *Community and Society: Gemeinschaft und Gesellschaft*. New York: Harper and Row.

Toohey, K. and Veal, A. (2000) *The Olympic Games: A Social Science Perspective*. Wallingford: CABI Publishing.

Tuan, Y. (1977) *Space and Place: The Perspective of Experience*. Minneapolis: University of Minnesota Press.

Turner, V. (1969) *The Ritual Process*. Harmondsworth: Penguin.

Turner, V. (1987) *The Anthropology of Performance*. In V. Turner (ed.) *The Anthropology of Performance*. New York: PAJ Publications.

Tyler, M. and Hancock, P. (2001) 'Flight Attendance and the Management of Gendered "Organizational Bodies"', in K. Backett-Milburn and L. McKie (eds) *Constructing Gendered Bodies*. Basingstoke: Palgrave, 25–38.

Urry, J. (1990) *The Tourist Gaze*, 1st edn, London: Sage.

Urry, J. (2002) *The Tourist Gaze*, 2nd edn, London: Sage.

Urry, J. and Larsen, J. (2011) *The Tourist Gaze 3.0*, 3rd edn. London: Sage.

Van Gennep, A. (1960) *The Rites of Passage*. Chicago: Chicago University Press.

Veblen, T. (1925 [1899]) *The Theory of the Leisure Class: An Economic Study of Institutions*. London, George, Allen and Unwin.

Wagner, S. (1997) *Understanding Green Consumer Behaviour: A Qualitative Cognitive Approach*. London: Routledge.

Walker, P. (2008) 'Beijing Olympics Open with Spectacular Ceremony', *The Guardian*, 8 August. Available at: http://www.guardian.co.uk/sport/2008/aug/08/olympics2008.china1 (accessed May 2012).

Walo, M., Bull, A. and Breen, H. (1996) 'Achieving Economic Benefits at Local Events: A Case Study of a Local Sports Event', *Festival Management and Event Tourism*, 4(3–4): 95–106.

Warde, A. (1996) 'Afterword: The Future of the Sociology of Consumption', in *Consumption Matters*. Oxford: Blackwell.

Webber, D. (2004) 'Understanding Charity Fundraising Events', *International Journal of Nonprofit and Voluntary Sector Marketing*, 9(2): 122–34.

Wensing, H. and Bruce, T. (2003) 'Bending Rules: Media Representations of Gender During and International Sporting Event', *International Review for the Sociology of Sport*, 38(4): 387–96.

Westwood, J. (1997) *Sacred Journeys: Paths for the New Pilgrim*. London: Gaia Books.

Whitby Gazette (2011) 'Goth Chief Backing for Churchyard Ban', 10 October.

Whitby Goth Festival (2012) Photography Press Release, 3 April. Available at: www.whitbygothweekend.co.uk/news.php?item=36 (accessed June 2012).

Winge, T. (2006) 'Costuming the Imagination: Origins of Anime and Manga Cosplay', in F. Lunning (ed.) *Mechademia 1: Emerging Worlds of Anime and Manga*. Minneapolis: University of Minnesota Press, 65–77.

Wood, H. (1982) 'Festivity and Social Change'. London: Leisure in the Eighties Research Unit, Polytechnic of the South Bank.

Wylie, J. (2009) 'Landscape', in D. Gregory, R. Johnston, G. Pratt, M. Watts and S. Whatmore (eds) *The Dictionary of Human Geography*. Chichester: Wiley-Blackwell, 409–11.

Xiao, Q. (2011) 'Yoghurt and Dreams', *International Herald Tribune*, 23 May. Available at: http://www.freetibet.org/files/Chinawatch%20page%20on%20religion.pdf (accessed May 2012).

Yeoman, I., Robertson, M., Ali-Knight, J., Drummond, S. and McMahon-Beattie, U. (2004) *Festival and Events Management: An International Arts and Culture Perspective*. Oxford: Butterworth Heinemann.

Yuval-Davis, N. (2006) 'Belonging and the Politics of Belonging', *Patterns of Prejudice*, 40(3): 197–214.

INDEX